EASY PIANO

SIMPLE MOVIE SONGS

THE EASIEST
EASY PIANO SONGS

ISBN 978-1-5400-5518-7

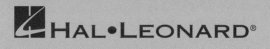

Visit Hal Leonard Online at
www.halleonard.com

Contact us:
Hal Leonard
7777 West Bluemound Road
Milwaukee, WI 53213
Email: info@halleonard.com

In Europe, contact:
Hal Leonard Europe Limited
42 Wigmore Street
Marylebone, London, W1U 2RN
Email: info@halleonardeurope.com

In Australia, contact:
Hal Leonard Australia Pty. Ltd.
4 Lentara Court
Cheltenham, Victoria, 3192 Australia
Email: info@halleonard.com.au

CONTENTS

CHARADE

from CHARADE

By HENRY MANCINI

Moderate Waltz

When we played our cha - rade,_____
Oh, what a hit we made,_____
Sad lit - tle ser - e - nade,_____

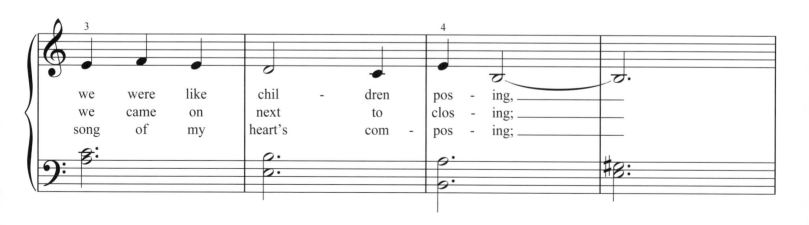

we were like chil - dren pos - ing,_____
we came on next to clos - ing;_____
song of my heart's com - pos - ing;_____

To Coda ⊕

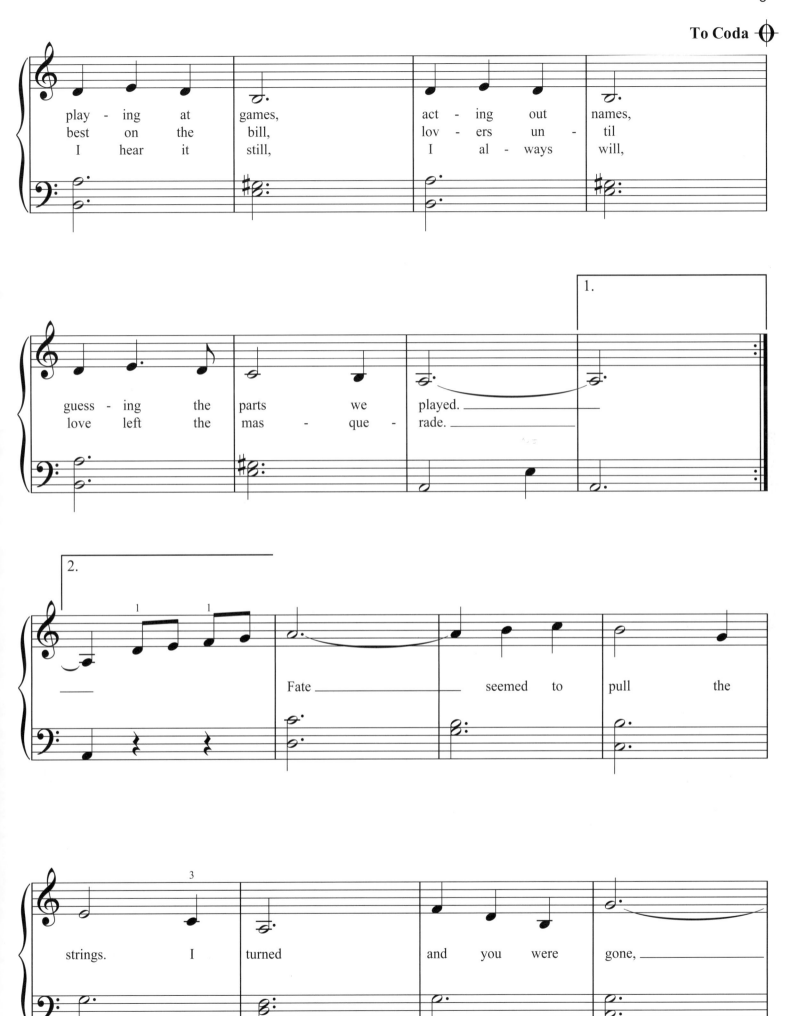

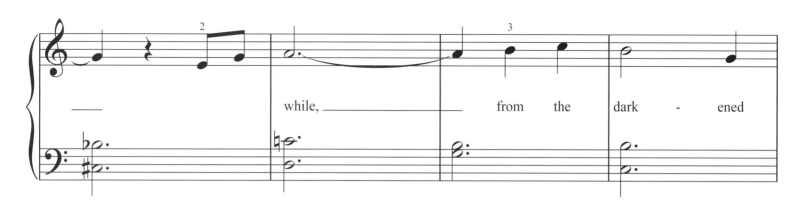

while, _____ from the dark - ened

D.S. al Coda

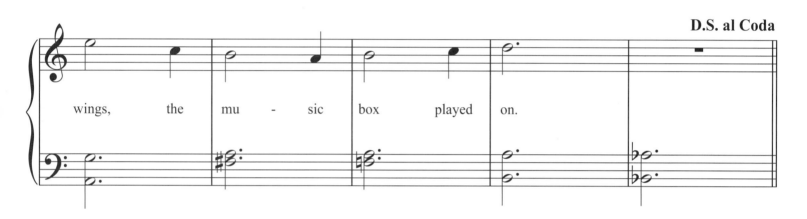

wings, the mu - sic box played on.

CODA

best on the bill, best on the bill, _____

_____ cha - rade.

AT LAST
from ORCHESTRA WIVES

Lyric by MACK GORDON
Music by HARRY WARREN

Slow Swing

mf

At

last____ my love____ has come a - long,____

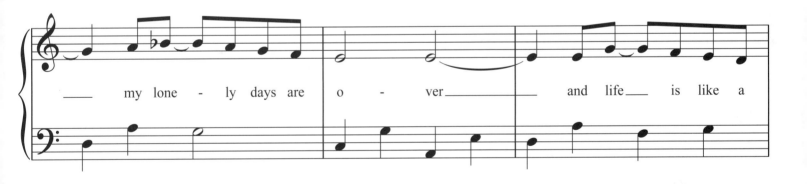

____ my lone - ly days are o - ver____ and life____ is like a

song.____ At last____

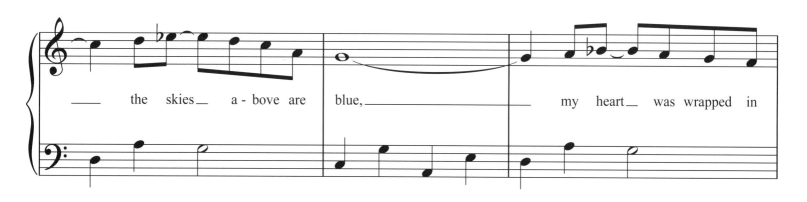

the skies___ a - bove are blue,_____ my heart___ was wrapped in

clo - ver_____ the night___ I looked at you._____

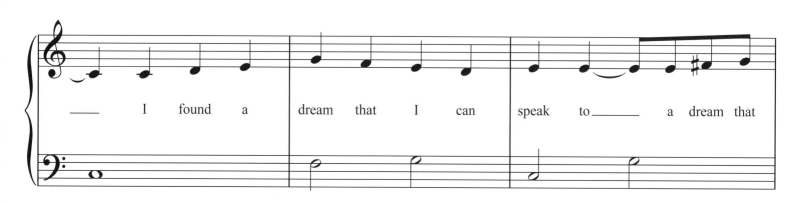

___ I found a dream that I can speak to_____ a dream that

I can call my own._____ I found a thrill to press my

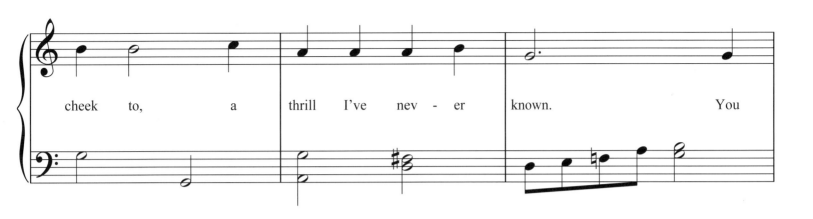

cheek to,   a   thrill I've nev - er   known.   You

smiled _____   and then ___ the spell was   cast _____

___ and here ___ we are in   heav - en _____   for you are mine at

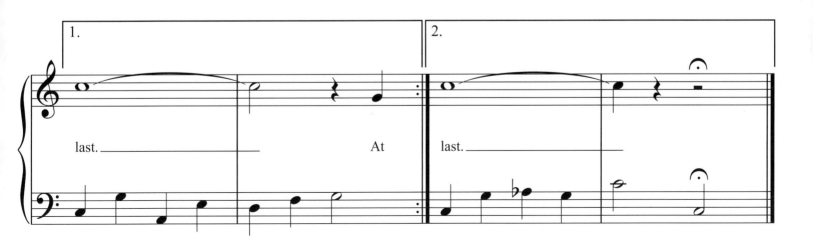

1.   2.
last. _____   At   last. _____

BORN FREE

from the Columbia Pictures' Release BORN FREE

Words by DON BLACK
Music by JOHN BARRY

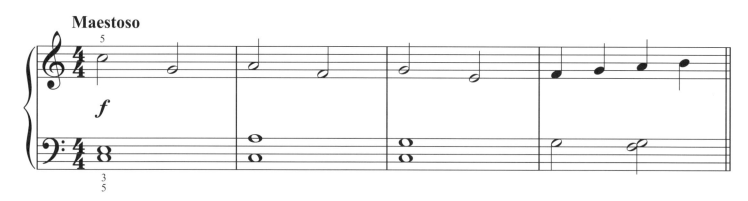

Born free, _____ as free as the wind blows, _____ as free as the
Live free, _____ and beau - ty sur - rounds you, _____ the world still as -

1.
grass grows, born free to fol - low your heart.

2.
tounds you each time you look at a star. _____ Stay free, _____

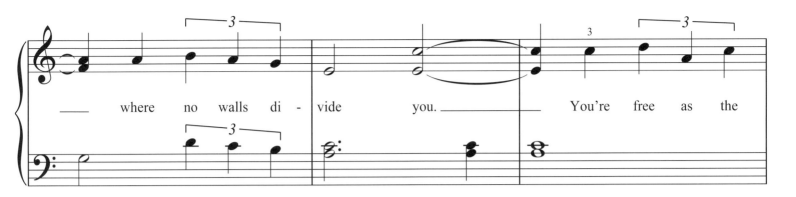

where no walls di - vide you. You're free as the

roar - ing tide, so there's no need to hide.

Born free, and life is worth liv - ing, but on - ly worth

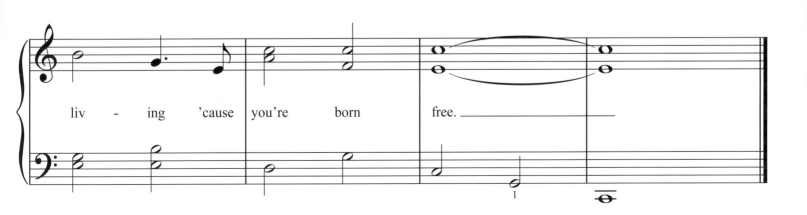

liv - ing 'cause you're born free.

CITY OF STARS
from LA LA LAND

Music by JUSTIN HURWITZ
Lyrics by BENJ PASEK & JUSTIN PAUL

Cit - y of stars, __ are you shin - ing just for

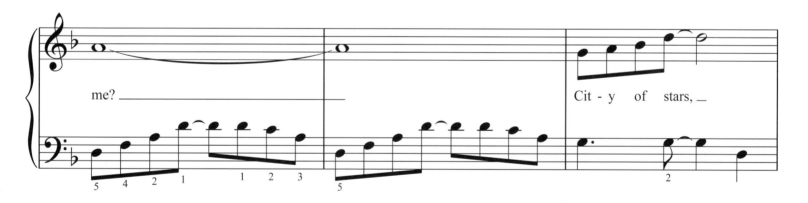

me? __ Cit - y of stars, __

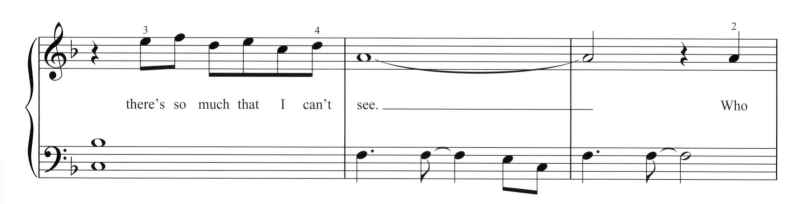

there's so much that I can't see. __ Who

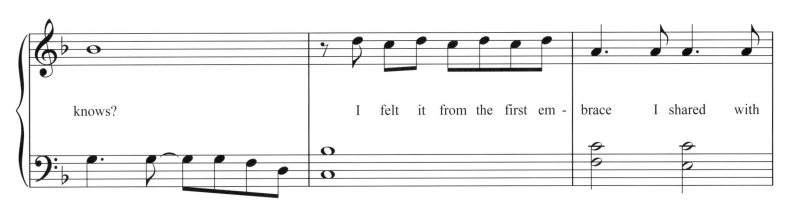

knows?   I felt it from the first em - brace   I shared with

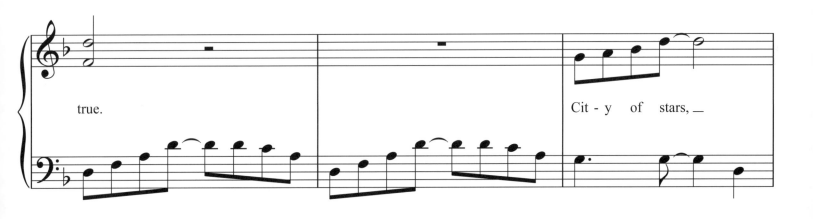

you   that   now   our   dreams   may   fi - n'lly   come

true.   Cit - y   of   stars, __

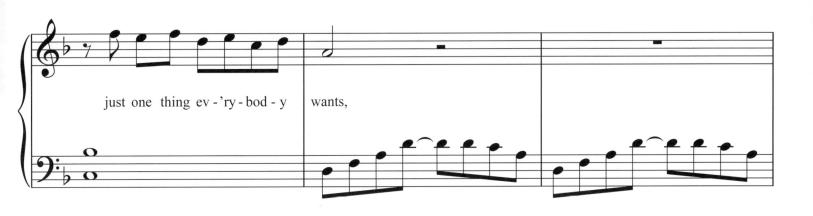

just one thing ev - 'ry - bod - y   wants,

14

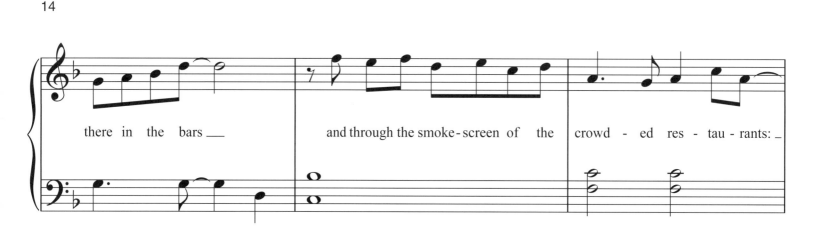

there in the bars ___ and through the smoke-screen of the crowd - ed res - tau - rants: _

___ it's love. Yes, all we're look - ing for is

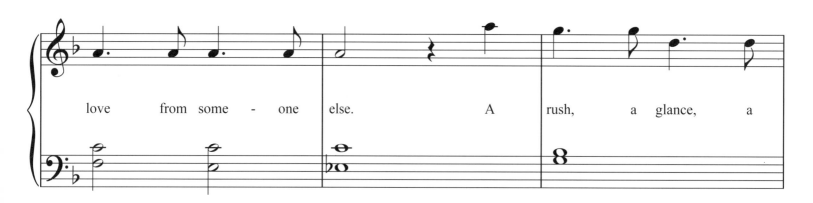

love from some - one else. A rush, a glance, a

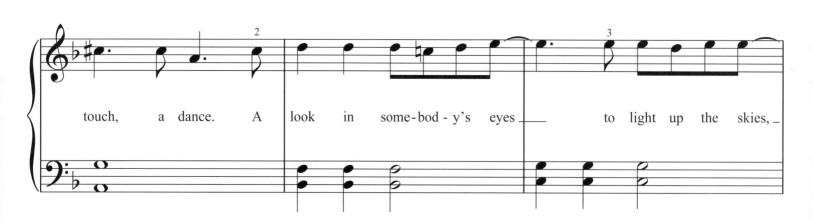

touch, a dance. A look in some-bod - y's eyes ___ to light up the skies, _

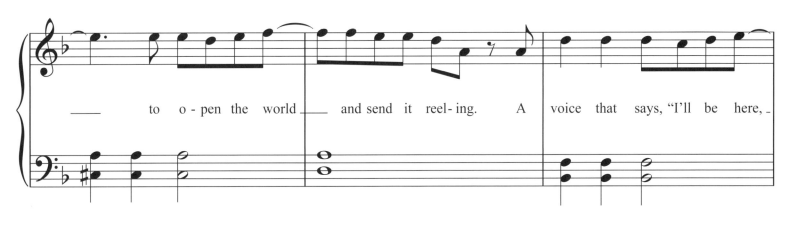

to o-pen the world ___ and send it reel-ing. A voice that says, "I'll be here, ___

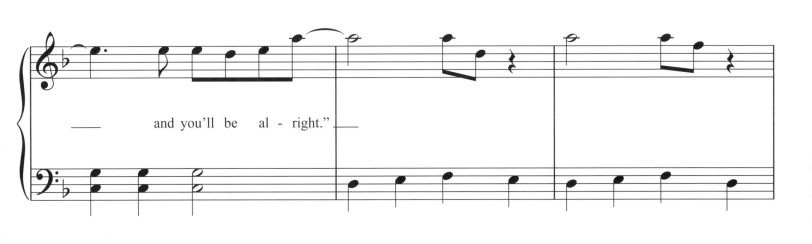

___ and you'll be al - right." ___

I don't care if I know ___ just where I will go, ___ 'cause all that I need's ___

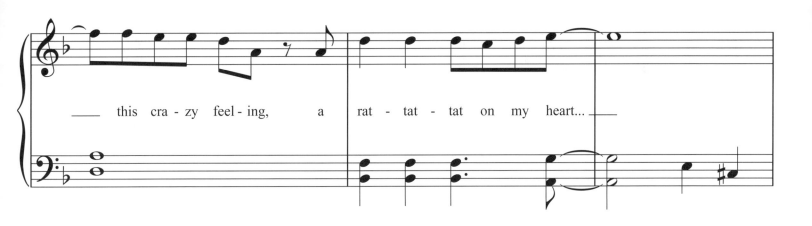

___ this cra - zy feel-ing, a rat - tat - tat on my heart... ___

Freely

Think I want it to stay. _____

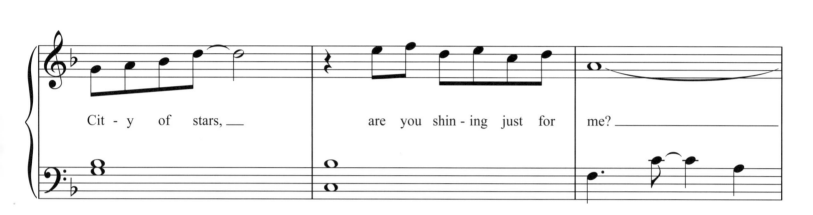

Cit - y of stars, ___ are you shin - ing just for me? _____

Slowly, freely

_____ Cit - y of stars, ___ you nev - er shined so

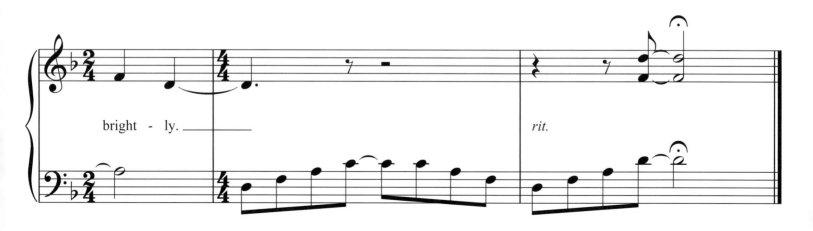

bright - ly. _____ _____ *rit.*

CUPS
(When I'm Gone)
from the Motion Picture Soundtrack PITCH PERFECT

Words and Music by A.P. CARTER,
LUISA GERSTEIN and HELOISE TUNSTALL-BEHRENS

Moderate Folk

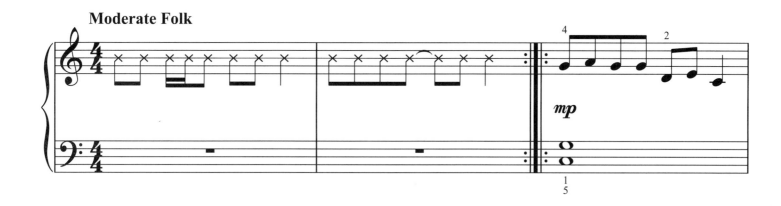

I got my tick - et for the long __ way 'round, __

two bot - tle o' whis - key for the way. And I sure would like __ some

sweet com - pa - ny. And I'm leav - in' to - mor - row, what do ya

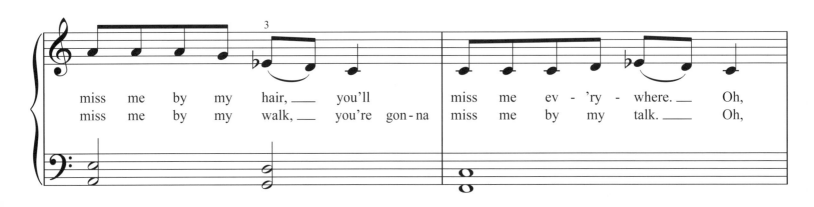

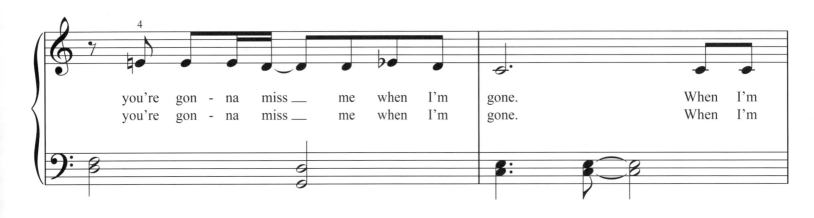

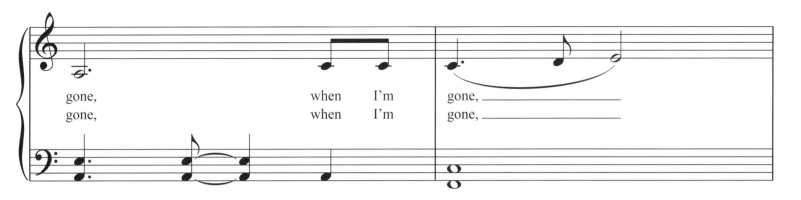

gone, when I'm gone,
gone, when I'm gone,

you're gon - na miss me when I'm gone. You're gon - na
you're gon - na miss me when I'm gone. You're gon - na

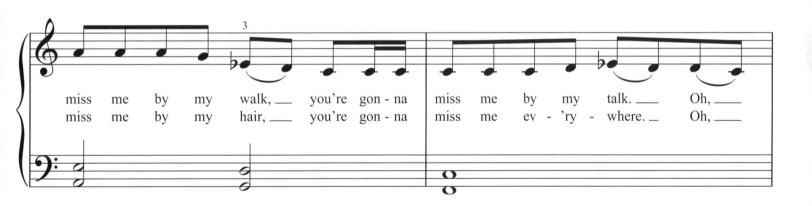

miss me by my walk, you're gon - na miss me by my talk. Oh,
miss me by my hair, you're gon - na miss me ev - 'ry - where. Oh,

To Coda ⊕

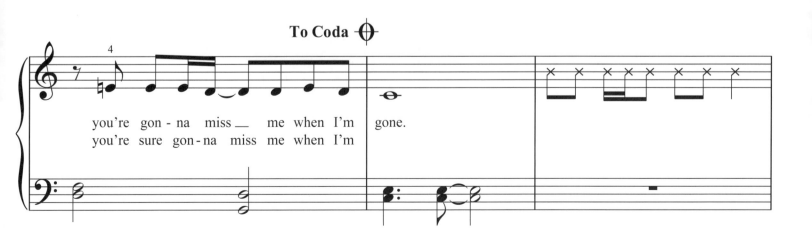

you're gon - na miss me when I'm gone.
you're sure gon - na miss me when I'm

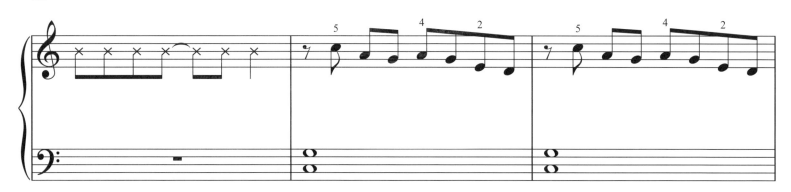

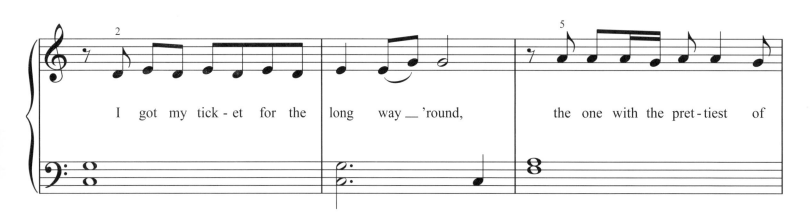

I got my tick - et for the long way _ 'round, the one with the pret - tiest of

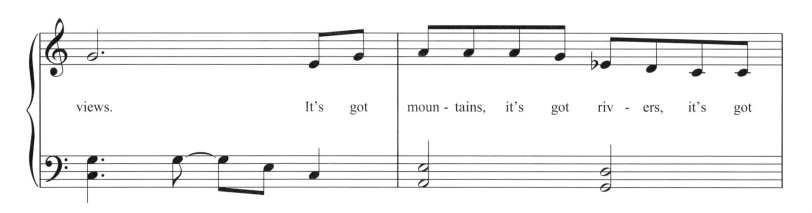

views. It's got moun - tains, it's got riv - ers, it's got

D.S. al Coda

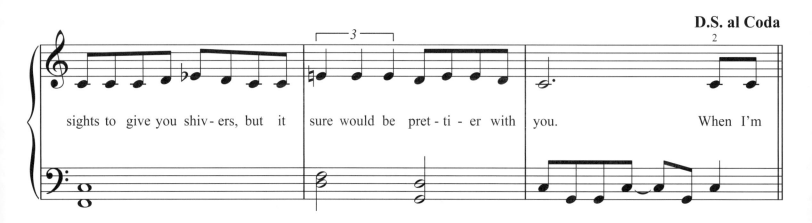

sights to give you shiv - ers, but it sure would be pret - ti - er with you. When I'm

CODA

gone.   When I'm   gone,   when I'm

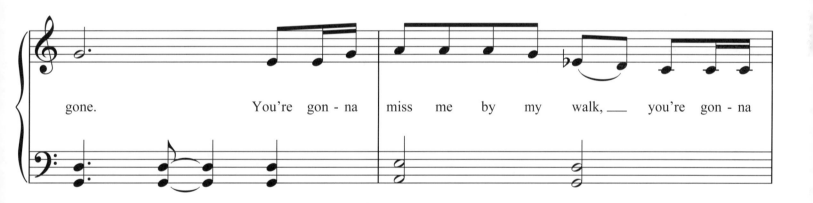

gone, _____   you're gon - na miss ___ me when I'm

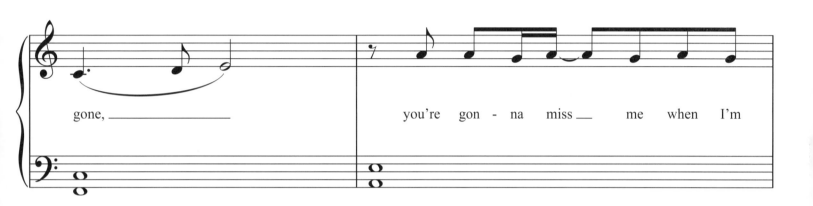

gone.   You're gon - na   miss   me   by   my   walk, ___   you're gon - na

miss me by my talk. ___ Oh,   you're gon - na miss ___ me when I'm   gone.

DANCING QUEEN
featured in MAMMA MIA!

Words and Music by BENNY ANDERSSON,
BJÖRN ULVAEUS and STIG ANDERSON

Disco Rock

You ____ can dance, ____ you ____ can jive, ____

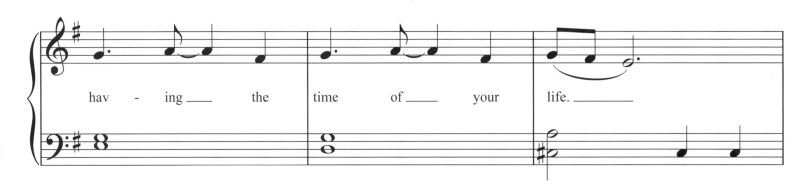

hav - ing ____ the time of ____ your life. ____

Oh, _____ see that ___ girl, ___

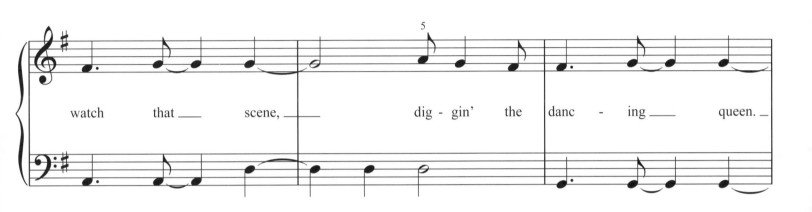

watch that ___ scene, ___ dig - gin' the danc - ing ___ queen. _

Fri - day night __ and the lights are low, _____

look - ing out __ for a place to go _____

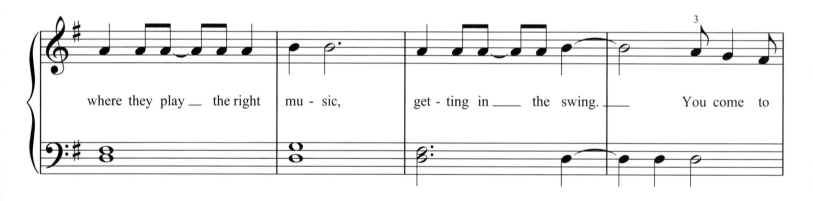

where they play __ the right mu - sic, get - ting in __ the swing. __ You come to

look for __ a king.

Anybody could be that guy.
You're a teas - er, you turn 'em on.

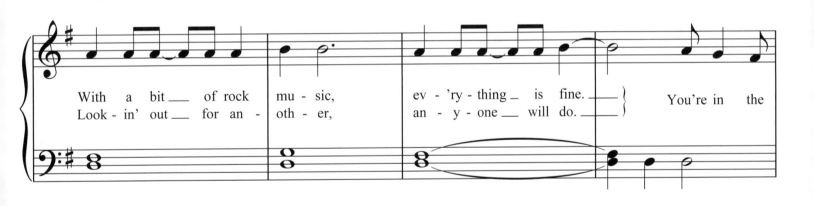

Night is young and the music's high.
Leave 'em burn - in' and then you're gone.

With a bit of rock music, ev-'ry-thing is fine. You're in the
Look - in' out for an - oth - er, an - y - one will do.

mood for a dance. And when you

tam - bour - ine, _____ oh yeah. _____

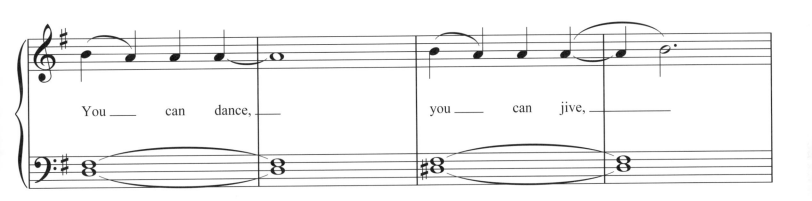

You ___ can dance, ____ you ___ can jive, ____

hav - ing ___ the time of ___ your life. ____ Oh, _____

see that ___ girl, ____ watch that ___ scene, ____ dig - gin' the

To Coda ⊕

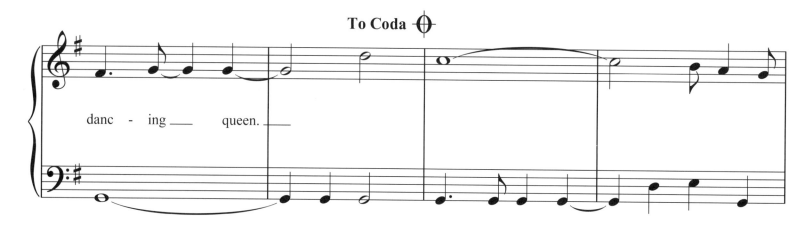

danc - ing —— queen. ——

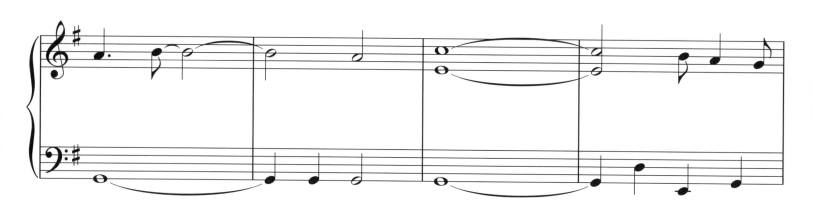

D.S. al Coda

CODA
⊕

DAWN
from PRIDE & PREJUDICE

By DARIO MARIANELLI

Moderately fast

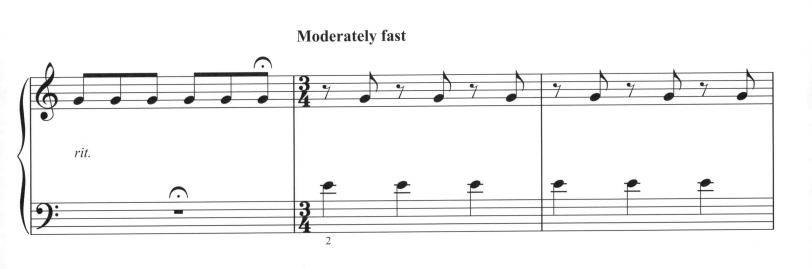

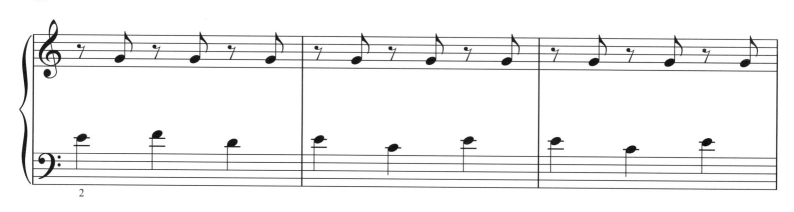

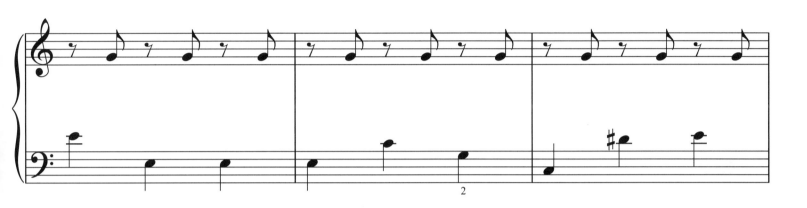

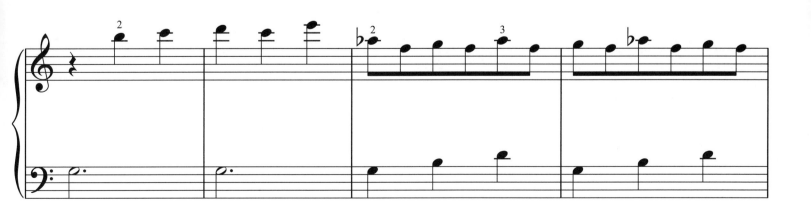

Slightly slower

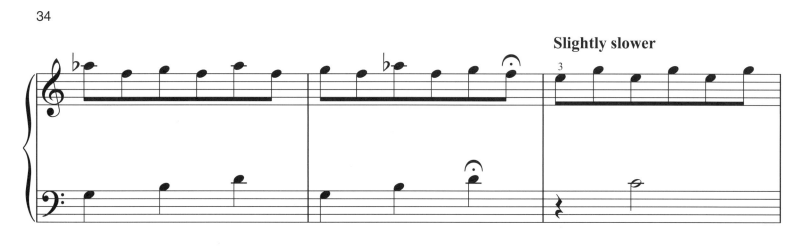

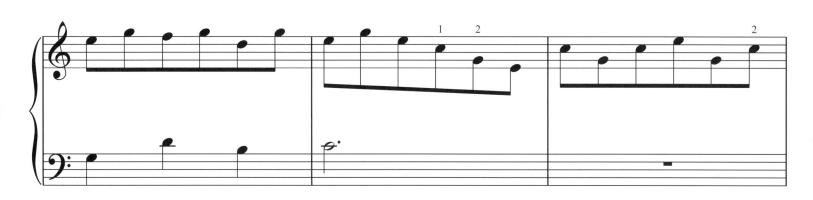

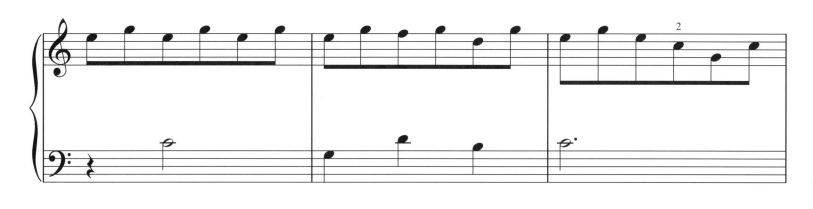

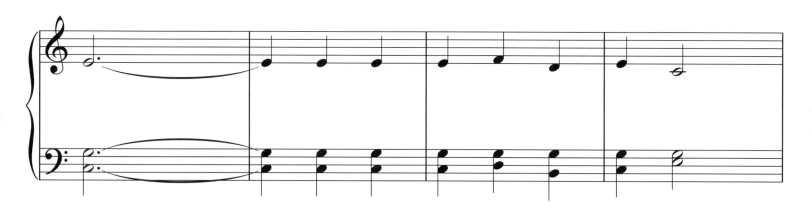

DAYS OF WINE AND ROSES

from DAYS OF WINE AND ROSES

Lyrics by JOHNNY MERCER
Music by HENRY MANCINI

Moderately

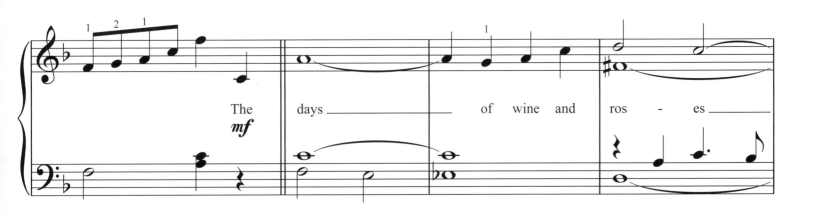

The days _____ of wine and ros - es _____

_____ laugh and run a - way _____ like a child at play _____

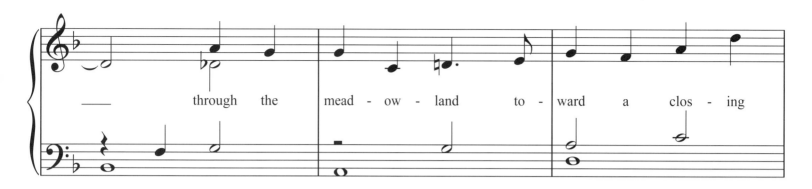

through the mead - ow - land to - ward a clos - ing

door, a door marked "Nev - er - more," that

was - n't there be - fore. _____ The lone

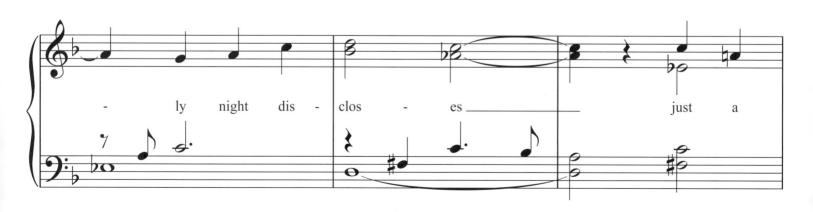

- ly night dis - clos - es _____ just a

passing breeze　　　filled with mem - o - ries _____

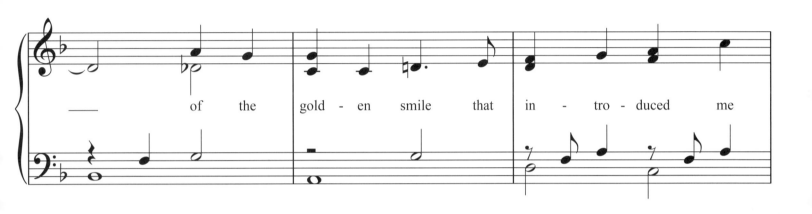

_____ of the gold - en smile that in - tro - duced me

to _____　　　the days of wine and

ros - es　and　you.　　*rit.*

THE DREAME
from the film SENSE AND SENSIBILITY

By PATRICK DOYLE

Moderately, with expression

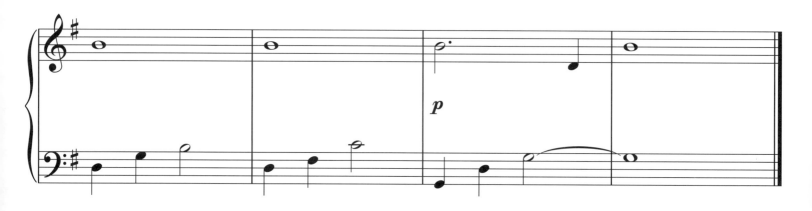

ENDLESS LOVE

from ENDLESS LOVE

Words and Music by
LIONEL RICHIE

step I make. ___
sist your charms. ___
And I,
And love,

I want to share all my love with
I'll be a fool for you. I'm

you, _____
sure _____
no one else
you ___ know
will ___ do. ___
I don't mind, ___

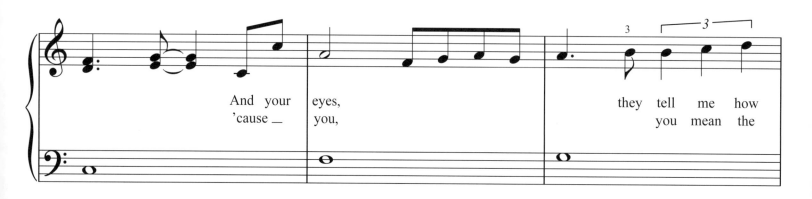

And your eyes,
'cause ___ you,
they tell me how
you mean the

EVERMORE
from BEAUTY AND THE BEAST

Music by ALAN MENKEN
Lyrics by TIM RICE

Moderately slow, with freedom

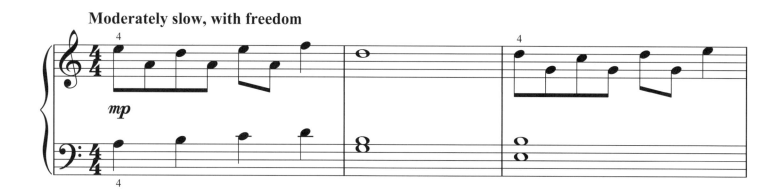

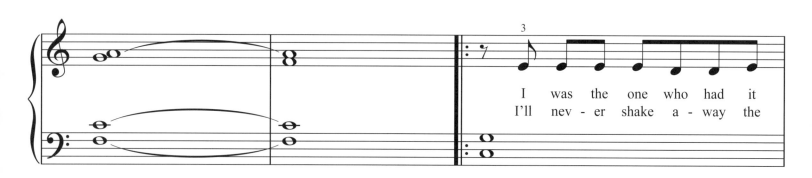

fate.
there.

I nev - er need - ed an - y - bod - y in my life;
I let her steal in - to my mel - an - chol - y heart;

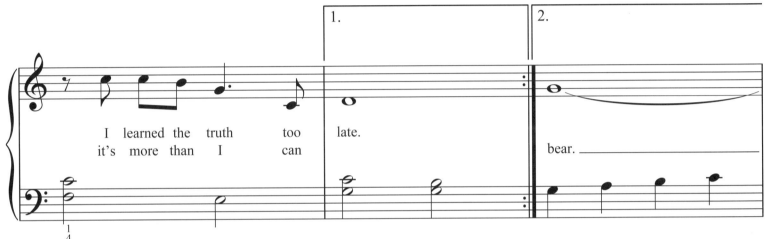

I learned the truth too late.
it's more than I can bear.

Now I know she'll nev - er leave me, e - ven

as she runs a - way. She will still tor - ment me,

calm me, hurt ___ me, move me, come what may.

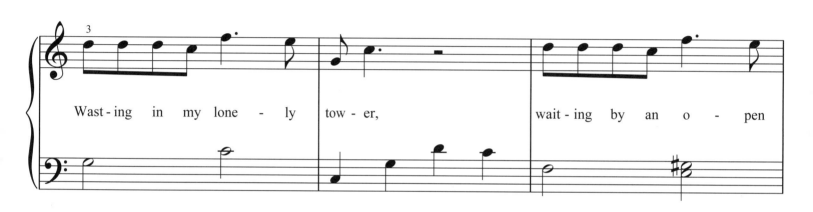

Wast - ing in my lone - ly tow - er, wait - ing by an o - pen

door, I'll fool my - self she'll walk right in,

and be with me for - ev - er - more.

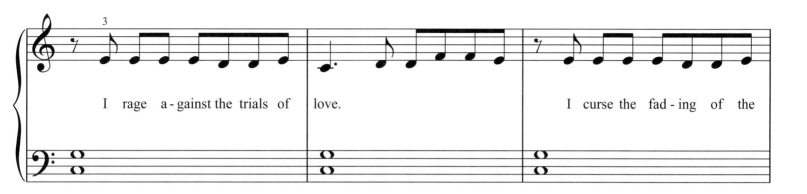

I rage a-gainst the trials of love. I curse the fad-ing of the

light. Though she's al-read-y flown so far be-yond my reach,

she's nev-er out of sight. Now I

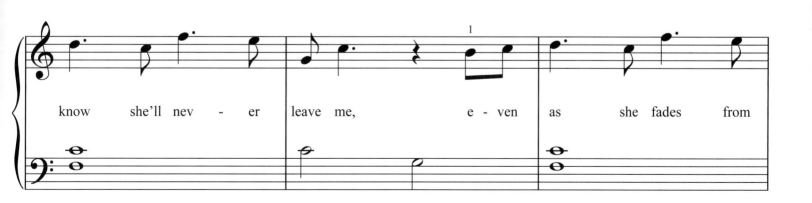

know she'll nev - er leave me, e - ven as she fades from

view.   She will still in - spire me,   be   a part ___ of

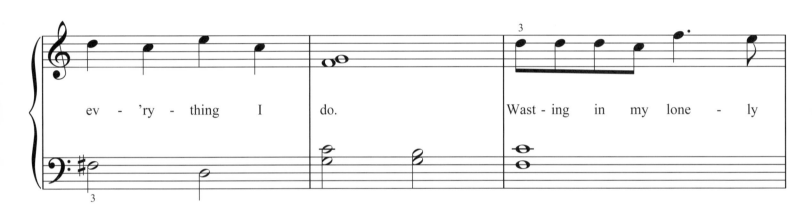

ev - 'ry - thing I   do.   Wast - ing in my lone - ly

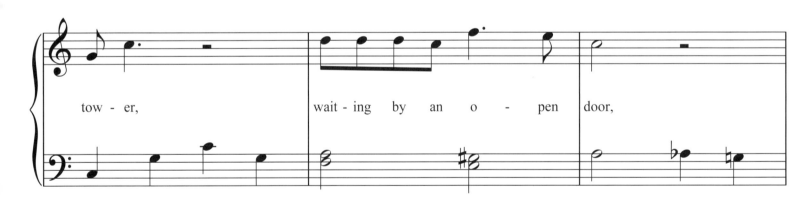

tow - er,   wait - ing by an o - pen door,

I'll fool my - self she'll walk right   in,

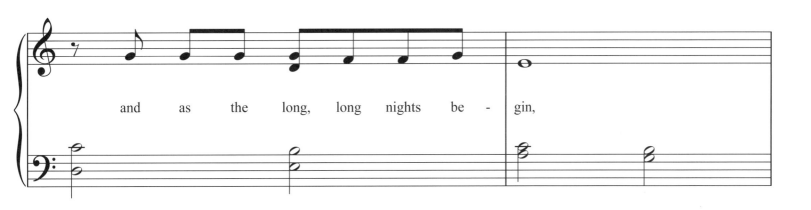

and   as   the   long,   long   nights   be - gin,

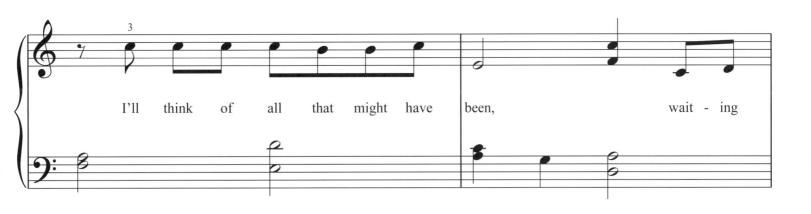

I'll   think   of   all   that   might   have   been,   wait - ing

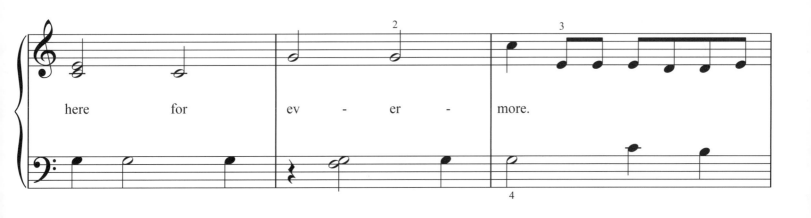

here   for   ev - er - more.

FALLING SLOWLY
from the Motion Picture ONCE

Words and Music by GLEN HANSARD
and MARKETA IRGLOVA

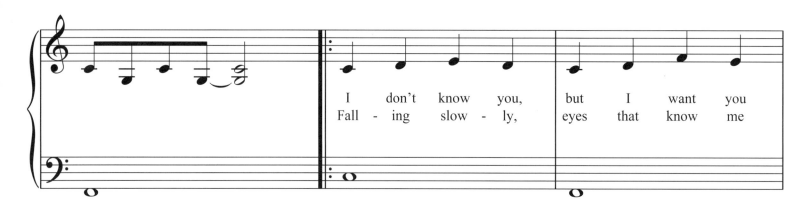

I don't know you, but I want you
Fall - ing slow - ly, eyes that know me

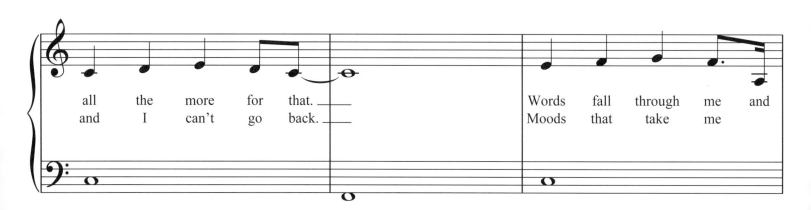

all the more for that.
and I can't go back.

Words fall through me and
Moods that take me

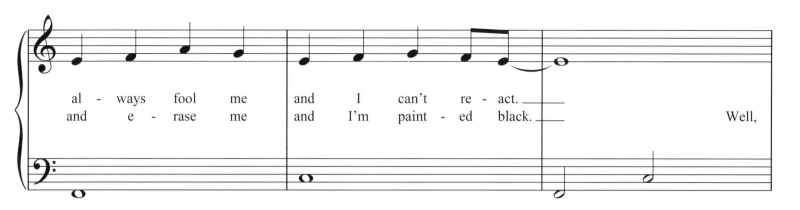

al - ways fool me and I can't re - act. ____
and e - rase me and I'm paint - ed black. ____ Well,

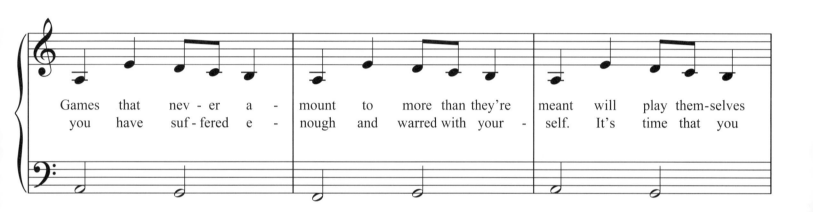

Games that nev - er a - mount to more than they're meant will play them-selves
you have suf - fered e - nough and warred with your - self. It's time that you

out. ____
won. ____

cresc.

Take this sink - in'

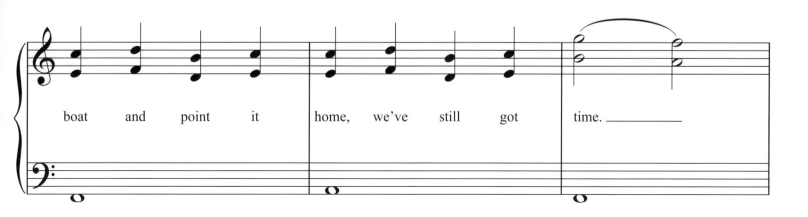

boat and point it home, we've still got time. ____

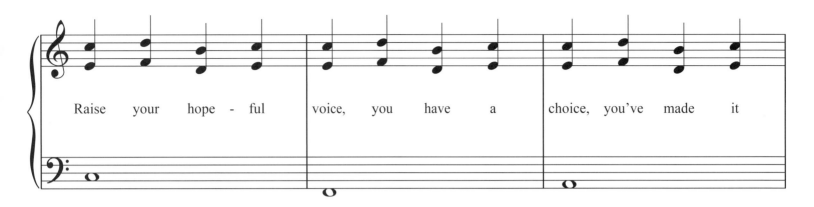

54

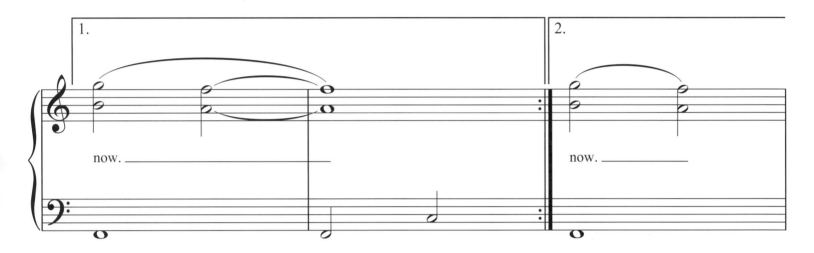

Raise your hope - ful voice, you have a choice, you've made it

1.

now.

2.

now.

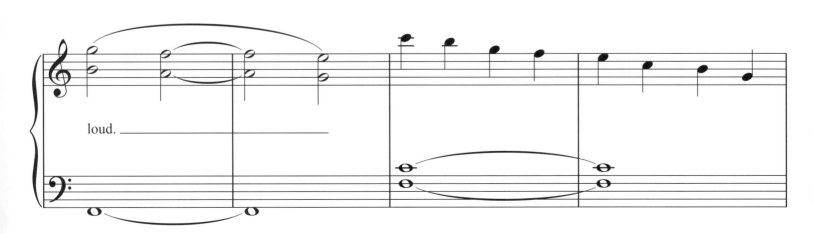

Fall - ing slow - ly, sing your mel - o - dy, I'll sing it

loud.

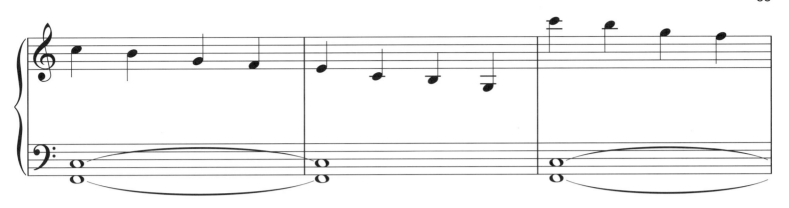

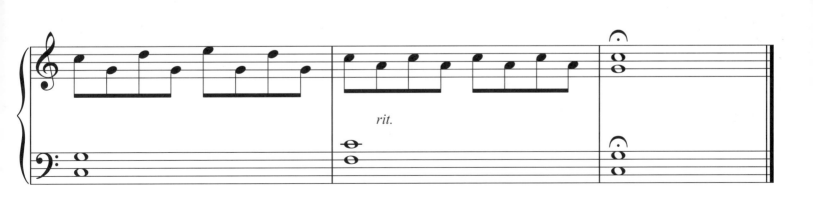

FROM NOW ON

from THE GREATEST SHOWMAN

Words and Music by BENJ PASEK
and JUSTIN PAUL

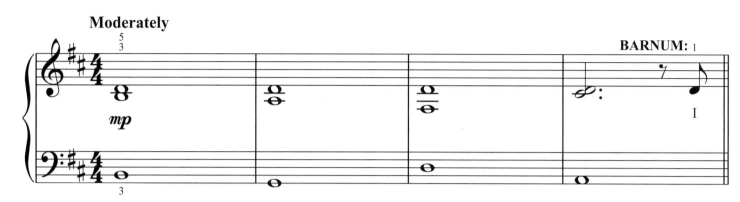

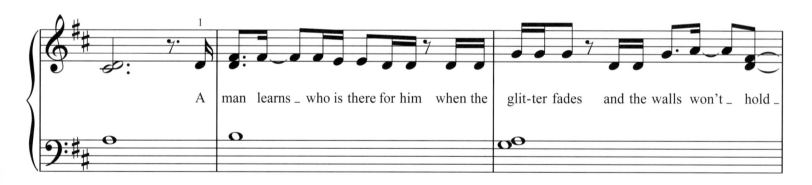

on - ly be ___ what's _ true   If all ___ was lost, there's more I ___ gained, _ 'cause it

led me ___ back   to you ___   From now

on   these eyes will not be blind - ed by ___ the lights

From now   on   what's wait - ed 'til to - mor - row starts to -

night,   to - night   Let   this   prom - ise   in   me   start   like   an

an - them   in   my   heart   from   now   on,   from   now

Moderately, in 2

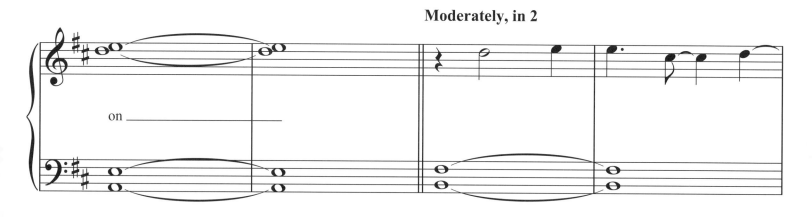

on

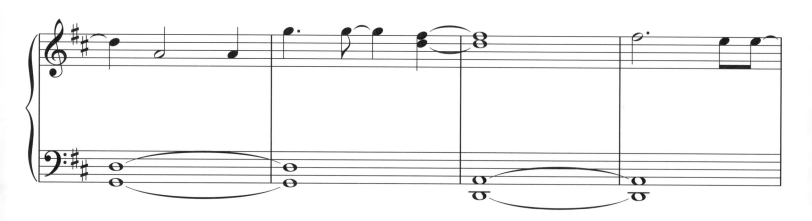

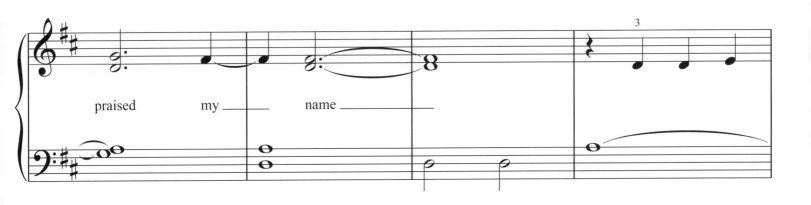

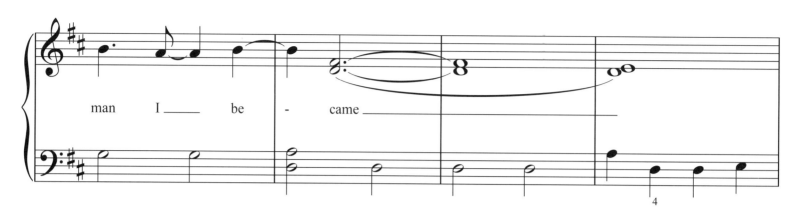

man I _____ be - came _____

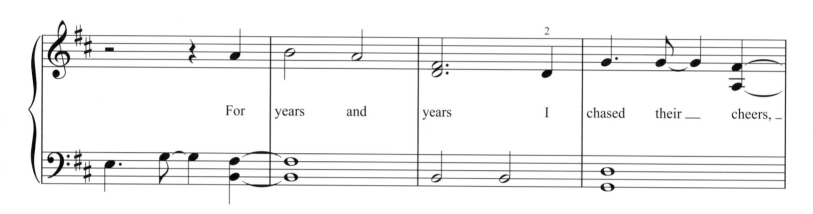

For years and years I chased their ___ cheers, ___

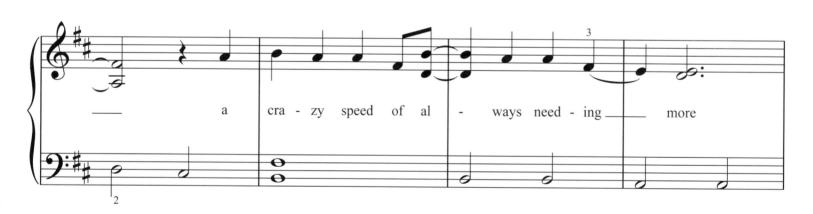

_____ a cra - zy speed of al - ways need - ing ____ more

But when I stop and ____ see you here

61

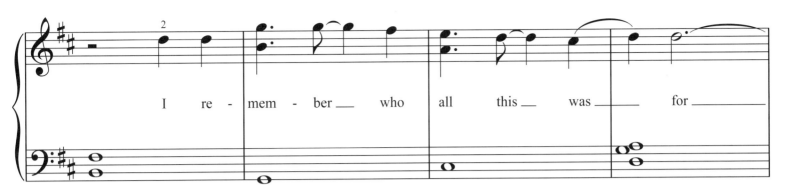

I re - mem - ber ___ who all this ___ was ___ for ___

___ And from now on

these eyes will not be blind - ed by ___ the lights

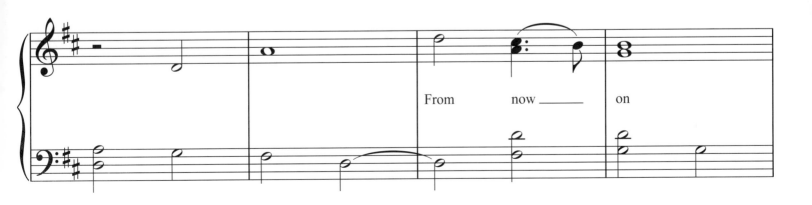

From now ___ on

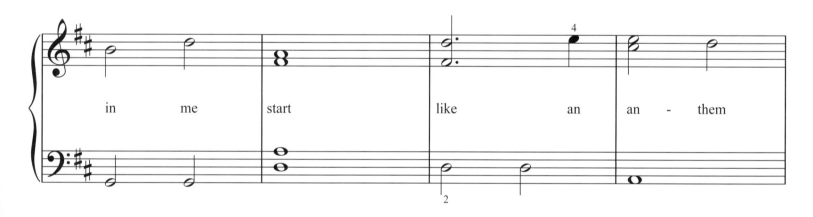

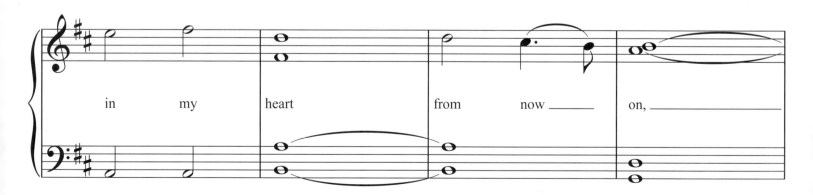

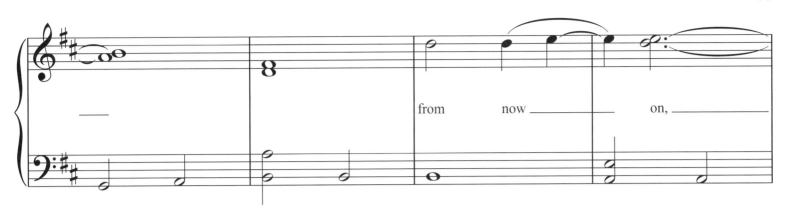

from now _____ on, _____

_____ from now on And we will

come back ___ home, and we will come back ___ home, ___

1.–3.   4.

home   a - gain ___

GABRIEL'S OBOE
from the Motion Picture THE MISSION

Music by
ENNIO MORRICONE

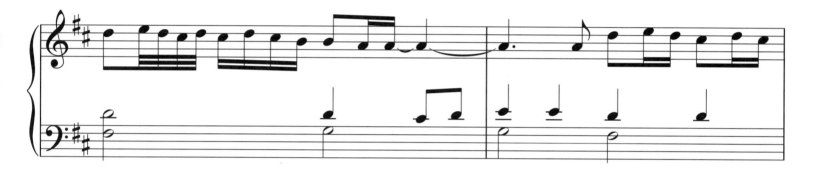

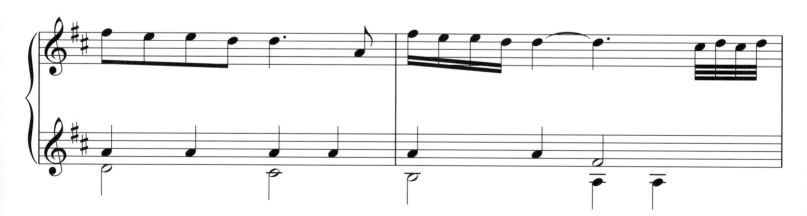

THE GODFATHER
(Love Theme)
from the Paramount Picture THE GODFATHER

By NINO ROTA

Slowly, with expresison

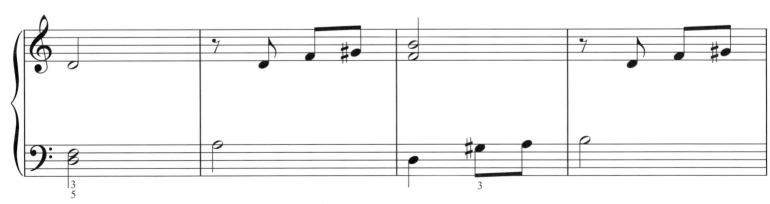

GOLDFINGER
from GOLDFINGER

Music by JOHN BARRY
Lyrics by LESLIE BRICUSSE
and ANTHONY NEWLEY

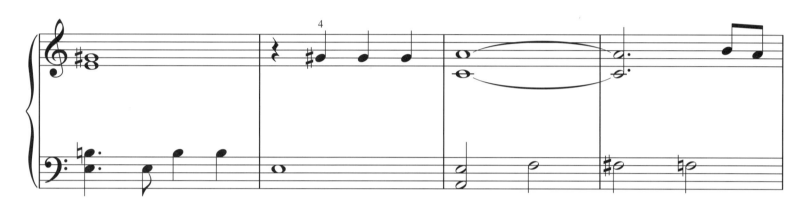

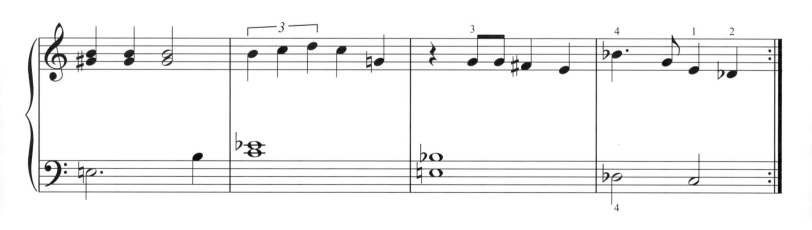

GONNA FLY NOW
Theme from ROCKY

By BILL CONTI,
AYN ROBBINS and CAROL CONNORS

Briskly

Try - ing   hard   now,

it's so hard now, ____ try-ing hard now.

Gon-na fly now, fly-ing

high now. Gon-na fly,

fly, fly!

I HAVE A DREAM

from MAMMA MIA!

Words and Music by BENNY ANDERSSON
and BJÖRN ULVAEUS

Easy Ballad style

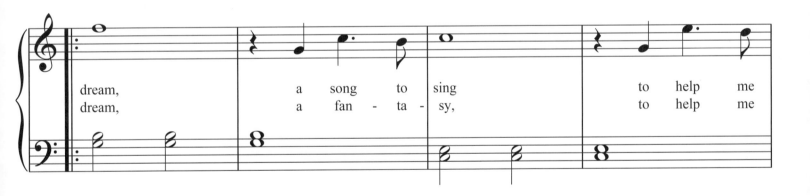

dream,   a song to sing   to help me

dream,   a fan - ta - sy,   to help me

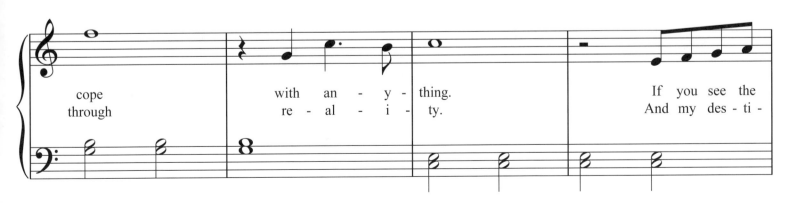

cope   with an - y - thing.   If you see the

through   re - al - i - ty.   And my des - ti -

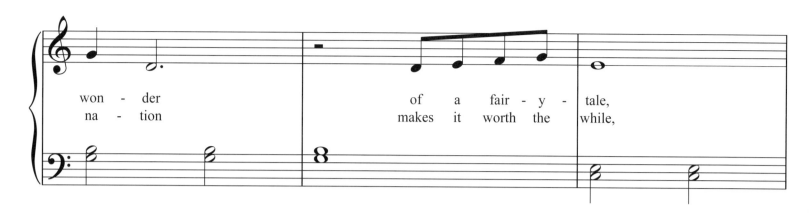

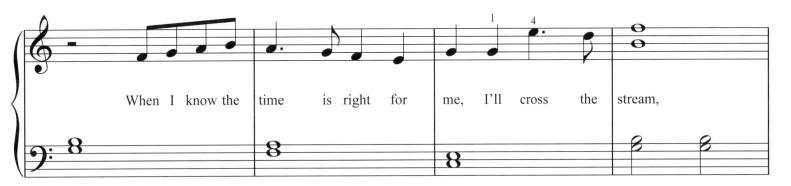

When I know the time is right for me, I'll cross the stream,

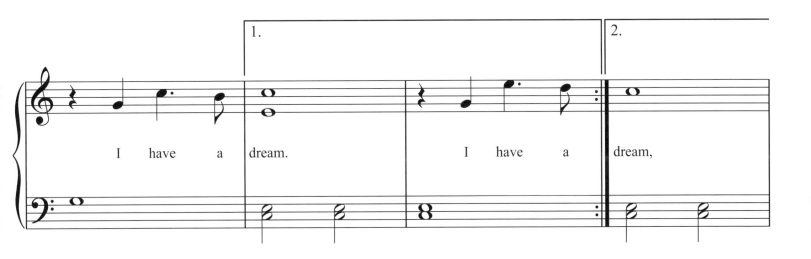

I have a dream. I have a dream,

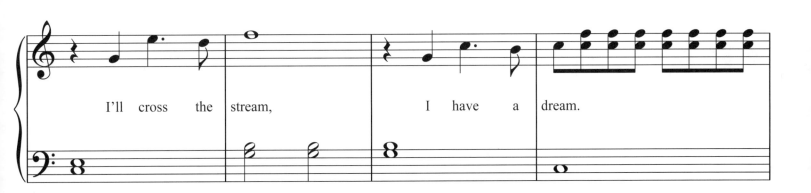

I'll cross the stream, I have a dream.

D.C. al Coda
(verse 1)

CODA

I be - lieve _____ in an - gels,

some-thing good in ev - 'ry-thing I see, I be - lieve in

an - gels. When I know the time is right for me, I'll cross the

stream, I have a dream, I'll cross the

stream,   I   have   a   dream, na na na na...

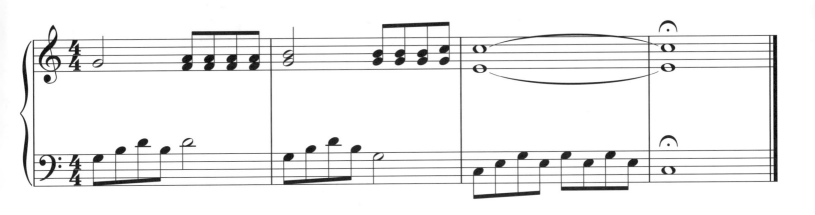

THE GOOD, THE BAD AND THE UGLY

(Main Title)
from THE GOOD, THE BAD AND THE UGLY

By ENNIO MORRICONE

Brightly, but not too fast

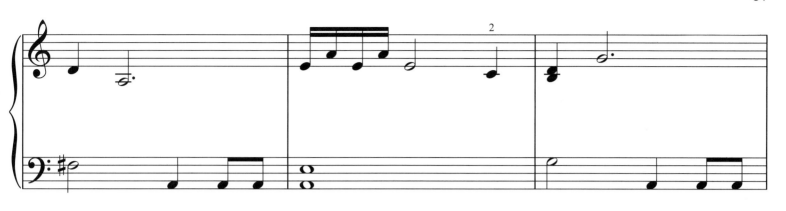

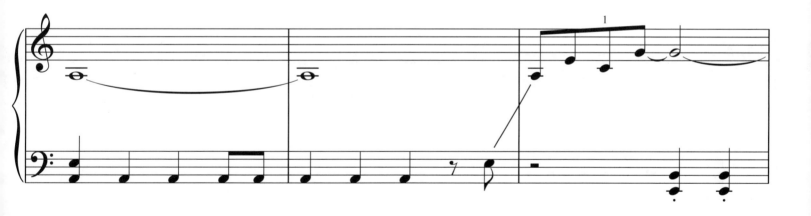

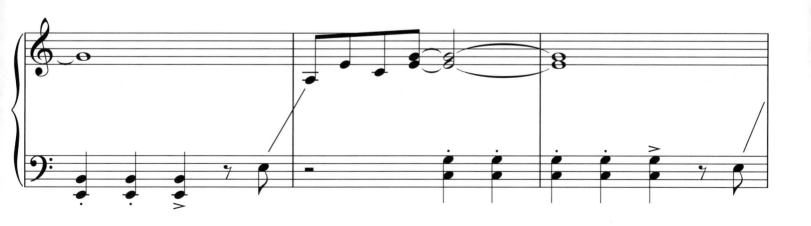

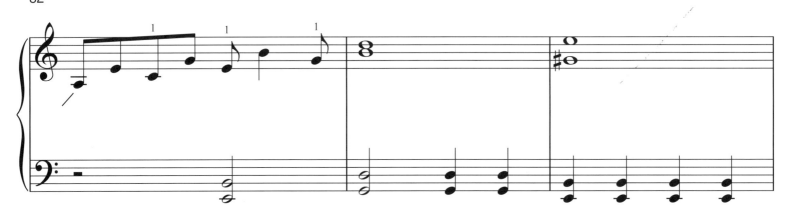

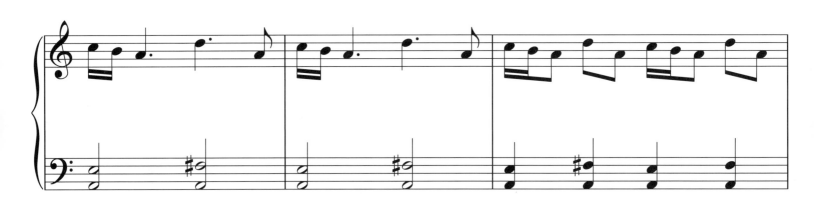

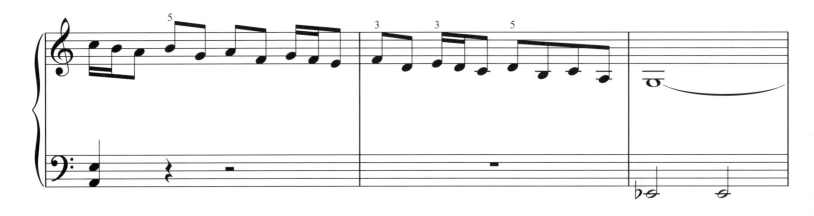

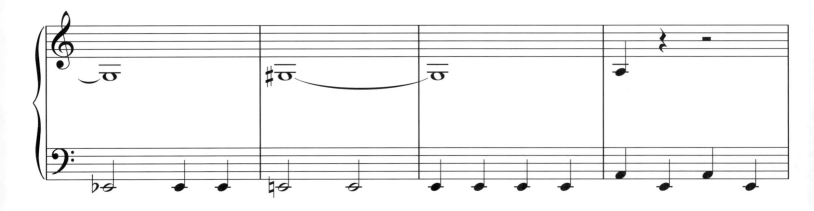

HAPPY
from DESPICABLE ME 2

Words and Music by
PHARRELL WILLIAMS

Moderately fast

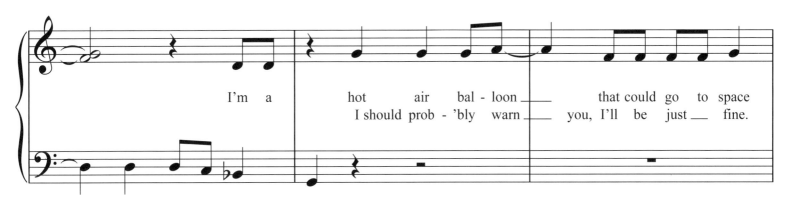

I'm a hot air bal - loon ____ that could go to space
I should prob - 'bly warn ____ you, I'll be just ____ fine.

with the air like I don't
No of - fense to

care, ba - by, by the way. ____ Huh!
you, don't ____ waste your time. ____ Here's why: ___

Be - cause I'm hap - py. ____
Clap a - long if you feel ____ like a

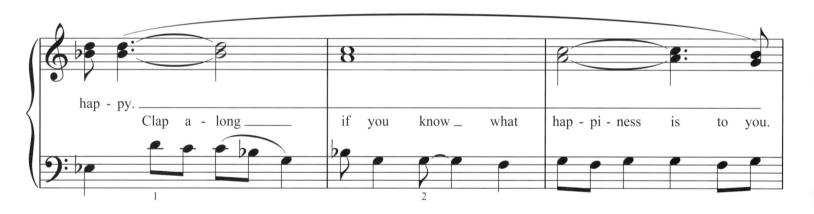

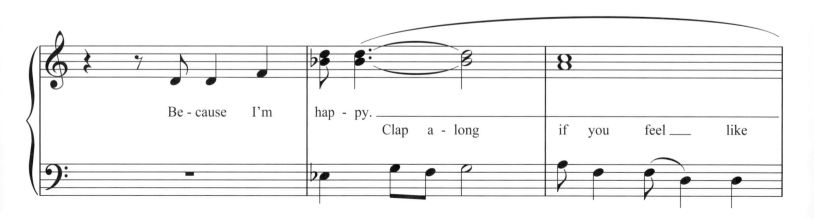

that's what you wan - na do.

Bring me   down, ____

____   can't noth - in'   bring me   down; ____   your love is too

high.   Bring me   down, ____   can't noth - in'   bring me   down. _

____   (Let me tell you now.)   Bring me   down, ____   can't noth - in'

bring me down; ___ your love is too high. Bring me down, __

__ can't noth - in' bring me down. __ Be - cause I'm

hap - py. _____
Clap a - long if you feel __ like a room with - out a roof.

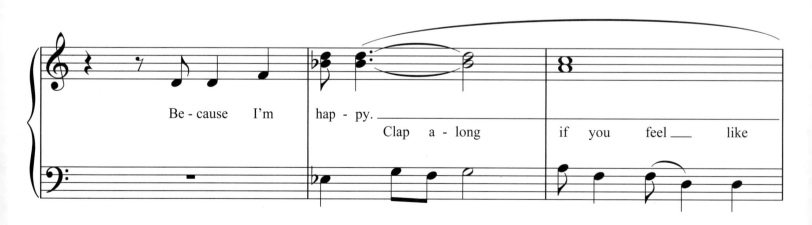

Be - cause I'm hap - py. _____
Clap a - long if you feel __ like

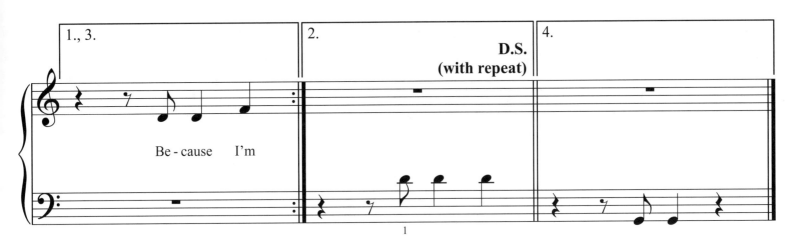

IF I ONLY HAD A BRAIN

from THE WIZARD OF OZ

Lyrics by E.Y. "YIP" HARBURG
Music by HAROLD ARLEN

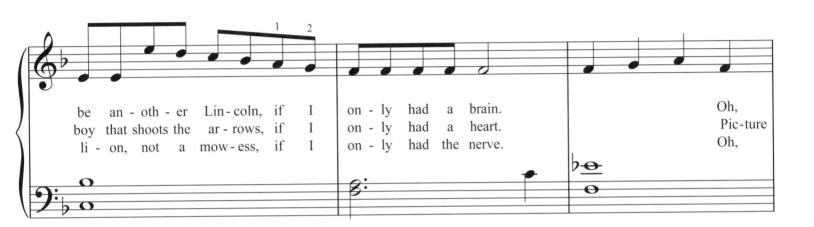

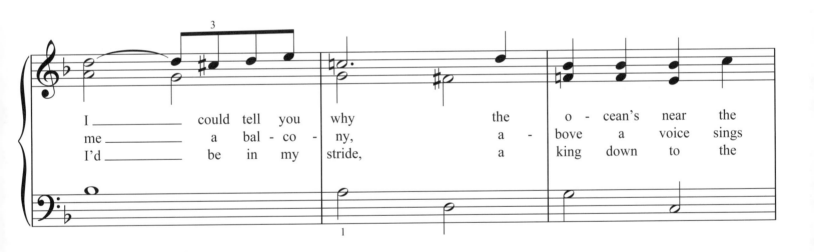

sit   and think some   more.   I would   not be just a nuff-in'   my
beat.   How   sweet!   Just to   reg-is-ter e-mo-tion,
rrrwoof,   and roar some   more.   I would   show the di-no-sau-rus   who's

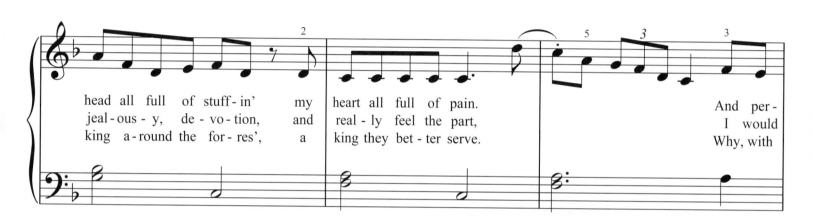

head all full of stuff-in'   my   heart all full of pain.   And per-
jeal-ous-y, de-vo-tion,   and   real-ly feel the part,   I would
king a-round the for-res',   a   king they bet-ter serve.   Why, with

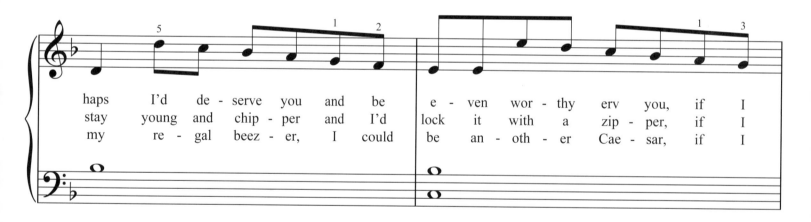

haps   I'd de-serve you   and   be   e-ven wor-thy erv you,   if   I
stay   young and chip-per   and   I'd   lock it with a zip-per,   if   I
my   re-gal beez-er,   I   could   be an-oth-er Cae-sar,   if   I

1., 2.   **3.**

on-ly had a brain.   When a   Life is
on-ly had a heart.
on-ly had the nerve.

JAMES BOND THEME

By MONTY NORMAN

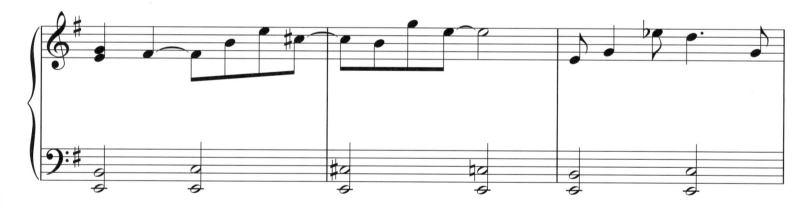

D.S. al Coda
(no repeat)

CODA

IT MIGHT BE YOU
Theme from TOOTSIE

Words by ALAN and MARILYN BERGMAN
Music by DAVE GRUSIN

Moderately slow

Time: I've been pass-ing time watch-ing

life, look-ing back as lov-ers go

trains go by. All of my life, ly-ing

walk-ing past. All of my life, won-d'ring

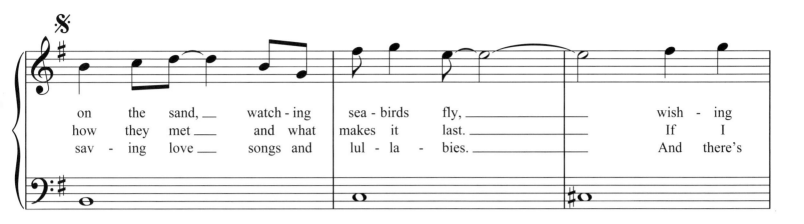

on the sand, __ watch - ing | sea - birds fly, _____ | wish - ing
how they met __ and what | makes it last. _____ | If I
sav - ing love __ songs and | lul - la - bies. _____ | And there's

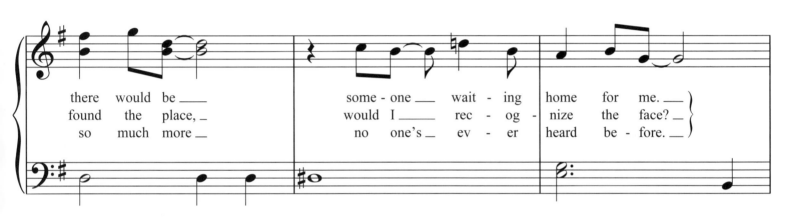

there would be __ | some - one __ wait - ing | home for me. __)
found the place, __ | would I ____ rec - og - nize | the face? __ }
so much more __ | no one's __ ev - er | heard be - fore. __)

Some-thing's tell - ing me it might be you. __ | | It's

To Coda ⊕

1.

2.

tell - ing me it might be you. __ | All of my |

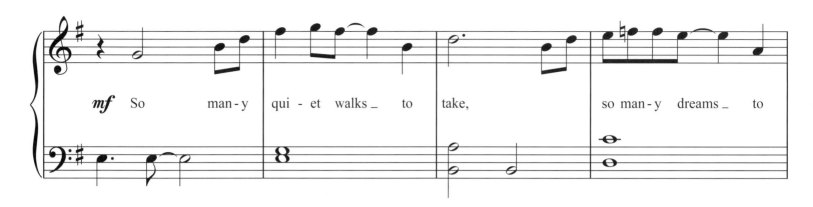

So man-y qui-et walks _ to take, so man-y dreams _ to

wake, and we've so much love _ to make.

I think we're gon-na need _ some time. May-be all we need _ is

time. _ And it's tell-ing me it might be you, _ all of my

life.

D.S. al Coda

CODA

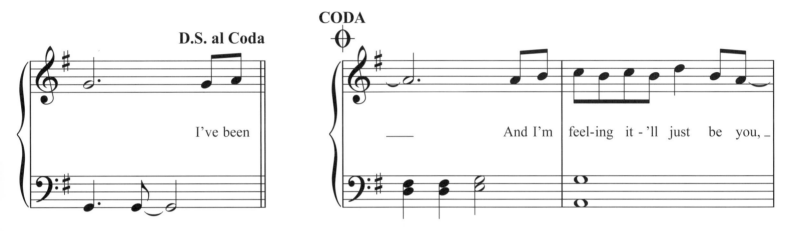

I've been

____ And I'm feel-ing it-'ll just be you, _

____ all of my life. May-be it's you, ___ may-be it's you _

1.

2.

____ I've been wait - ing for all of my - ing for all of my life.

rit.

THE MAGNIFICENT SEVEN

from THE MAGNIFICENT SEVEN

By ELMER BERNSTEIN

Moderately, with vigor

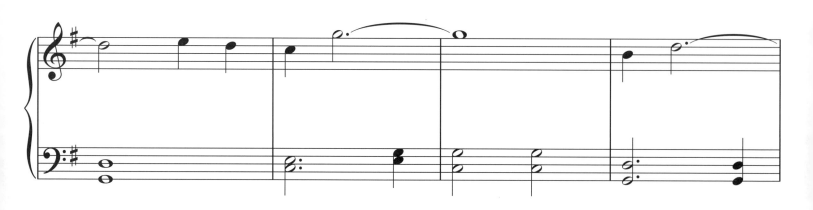

MIA & SEBASTIAN'S THEME
from LA LA LAND

Music by
JUSTIN HURWITZ

Moderately slow, expressively

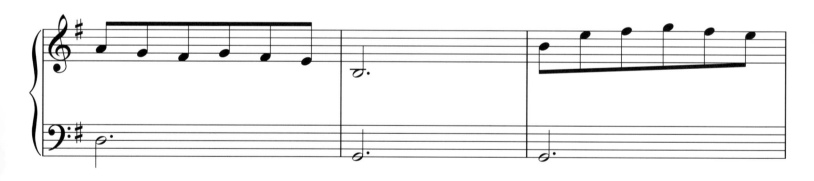

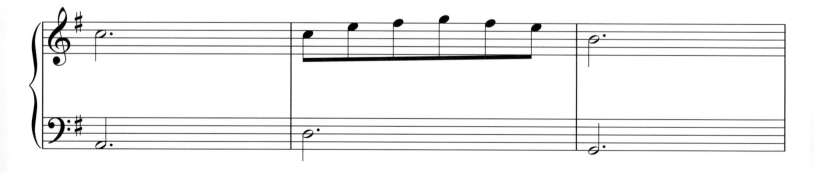

As fast as possible, freely

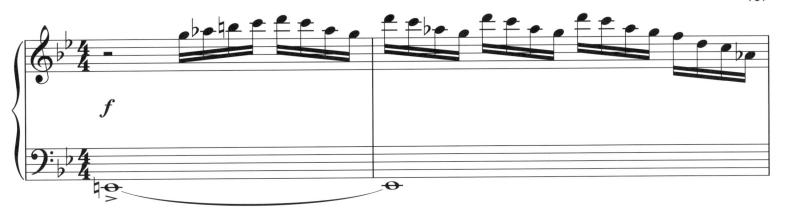

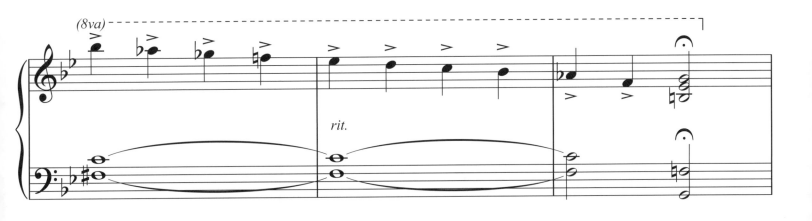

A MILLION DREAMS

from THE GREATEST SHOWMAN

Words and Music by BENJ PASEK
and JUSTIN PAUL

Moderately, with intensity

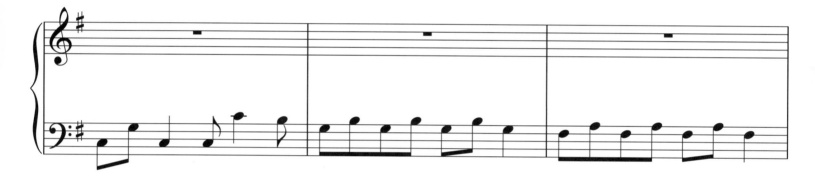

109

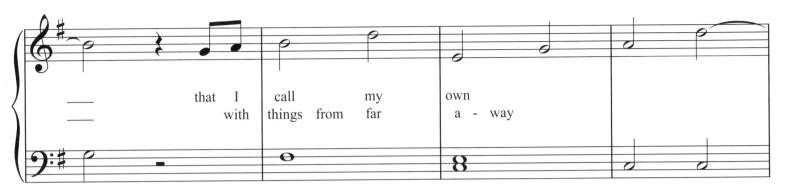

that I call my own
with things from far a - way

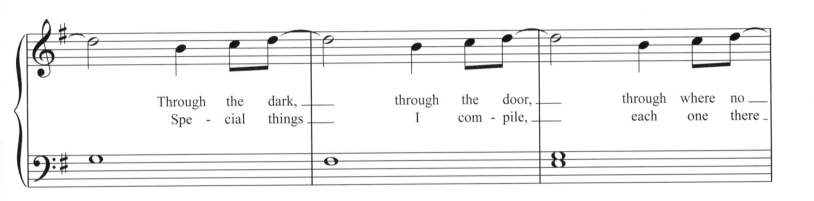

Through the dark, ____ through the door, ____ through where no ____
Spe - cial things ____ I com - pile, ____ each one there ____

____ one's been be - fore, ____ but it feels like home
____ to make you smile ____ on a rain - y day

They can say, they can say it all ____ sounds cra - zy
They can say, they can say it all ____ sounds cra - zy

They can say, they can say I've lost ___ my mind ___
They can say, they can say we've lost ___ our minds ___

I don't care, I don't care, so call me cra - zy
I don't care, I don't care if they call us cra - zy

We can live in a world that we ___ de - sign ___
Run a - way to a world that we ___ de - sign ___

'Cause ev - 'ry night ___ I lie ___ in bed ___ the

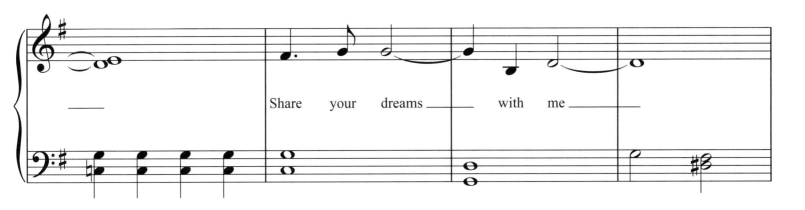

Share your dreams ____ with me ____

You may be right, ____ you may be wrong, ____ but say that you'll

bring me ____ a - long ____ to the world you ____ see, ____ To the

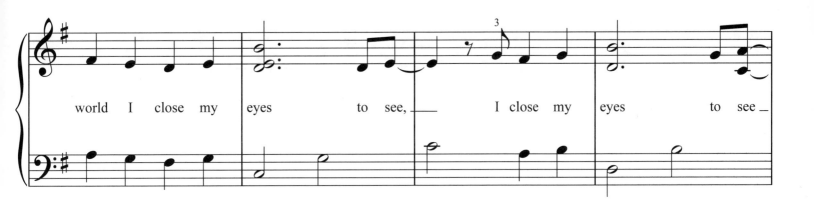

world I close my eyes to see, ____ I close my eyes to see ____

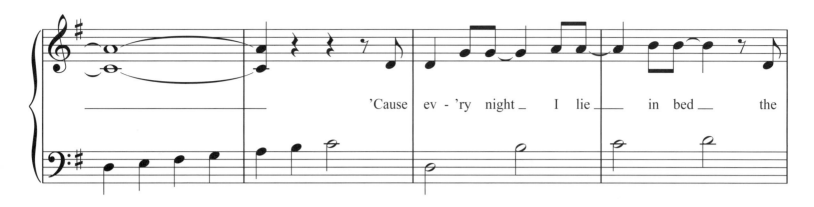

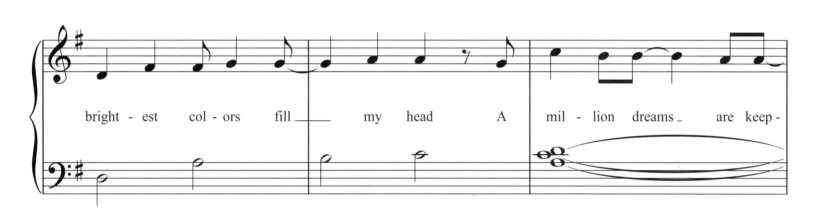

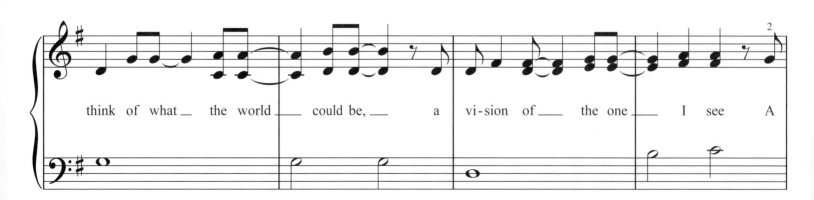

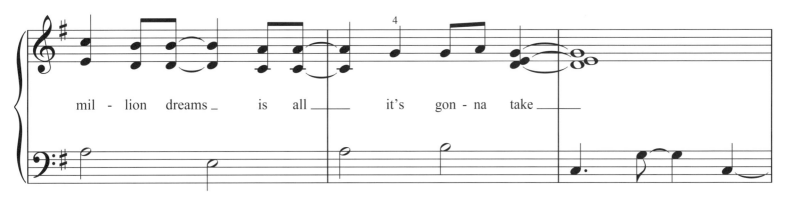

mil - lion dreams _ is all _ it's _ gon - na take _

A mil - lion dreams _ for the world we're gon - na make _

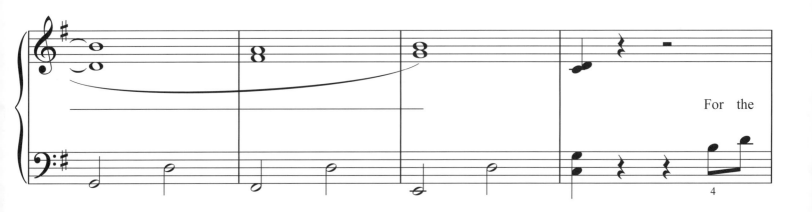

For the

Slowly, freely

world we're gon-na make

THE MUSIC OF GOODBYE
from OUT OF AFRICA

Words and Music by JOHN BARRY,
ALAN BERGMAN and MARILYN BERGMAN

Tenderly

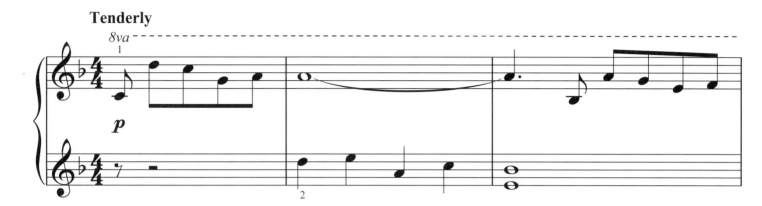

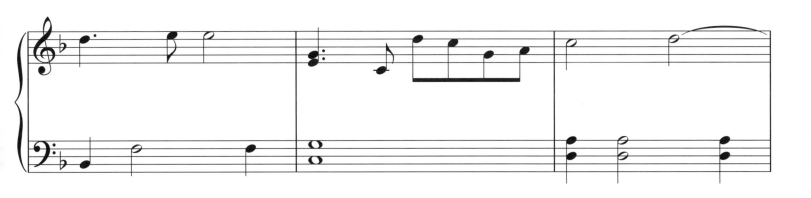

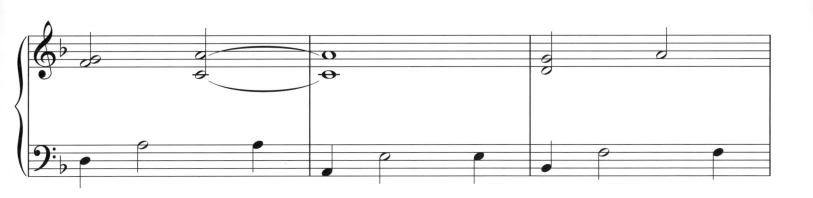

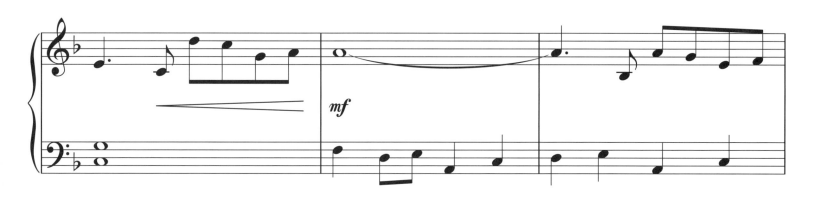

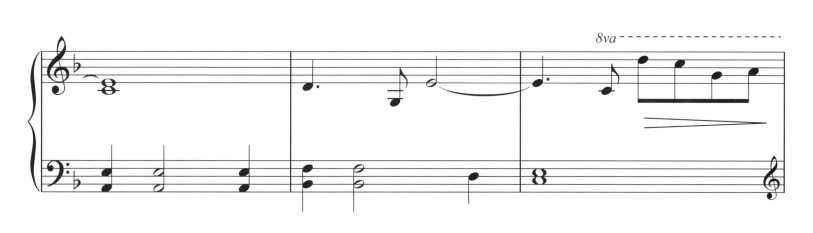

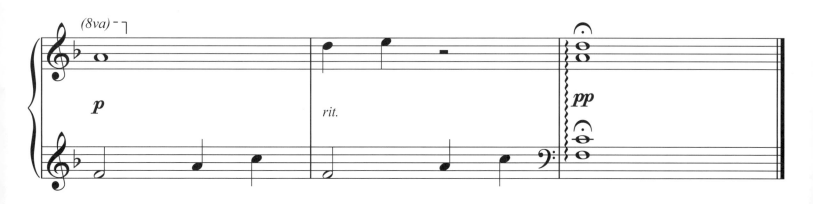

NEVER ENOUGH
from THE GREATEST SHOWMAN

Words and Music by BENJ PASEK
and JUSTIN PAUL

Will you share this with me? 'Cause dar - ling, with-out ___ you ___

all the shine of a thou-sand spot-lights, all the stars ___ we steal ___ from the night ___ sky will

nev - er be e - nough, ___ Nev - er be e - nough ___ Tow-ers of gold ___ are still too lit - tle These

hands could hold the world, but it - 'll nev - er be e - nough, ___ Nev - er be e -

nough ___   for me ___   Nev-er, nev-er   Nev-er, nev-er

Nev-er   for me ___   for me _   Nev-er e-nough _

Nev-er e-nough _   Nev-er e-nough _   for me, ___   for me, _   for me _

for me ___

THEME FROM
"NEW YORK, NEW YORK"

from NEW YORK, NEW YORK

Words by FRED EBB
Music by JOHN KANDER

Start spread-in' the news,   I'm leav-ing to-

day.   I wan-na be a part __ of it,

New York, New York. These vag - a - bond

shoes are long - ing to stray

and step a - round the heart ___ of it,
(D.S.) *Instrumental*
New York, New

York. ___
Instrumental ends
I wan - na wake up in the

124

city that does-n't sleep _____ to find I'm

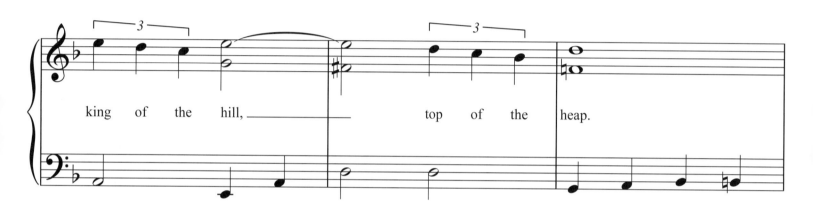

king of the hill, _____ top of the heap.

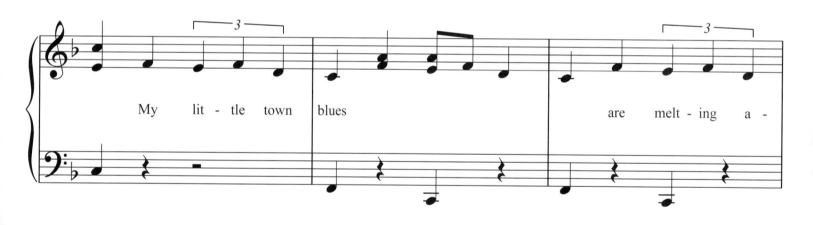

My lit-tle town blues _____ are melt-ing a-

way. I'll make a brand-new start __ of it

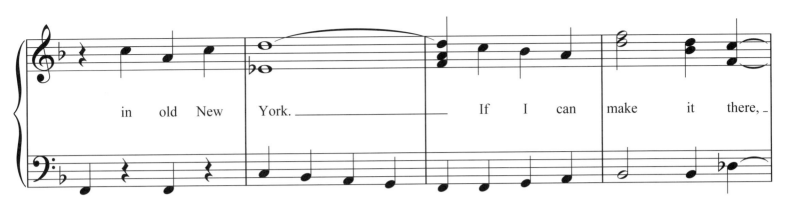

in old New York. _____ If I can make it there, _

_____ I'd make it an - y - where. _____ It's up to

you, New York, New York.

D.S. al Coda

CODA

king of the hill,   head of the list,   cream of the crop at the
rit.

Slower

top of the heap.   My lit - tle town   blues _____
molto rit.

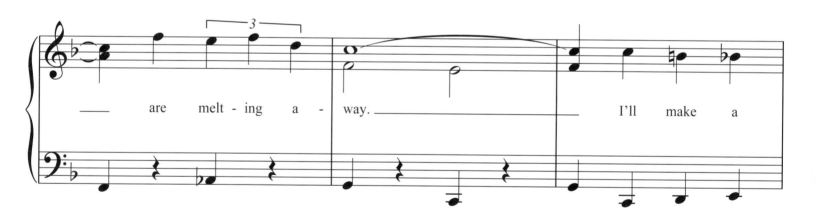

_____ are melt - ing a - way. _____   I'll make a

brand - new start ___ of it   in old New   York. _____

If I can make it there, _____ I'd make it

an - y - where. _____ Come on, come through, New

York, New York.

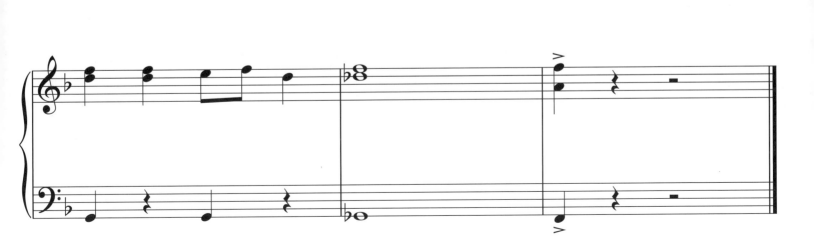

NOBODY DOES IT BETTER

from THE SPY WHO LOVED ME

Music by MARVIN HAMLISCH
Lyrics by CAROLE BAYER SAGER

best.
good?
I was-n't look-in'
The way that you hold me
but some-how you found me.
when-ev - er you hold me,

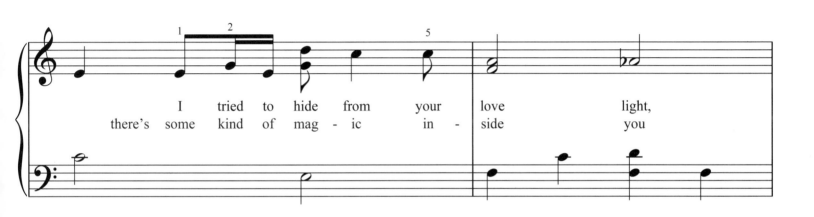

I tried to hide from your love light,
there's some kind of mag - ic in - side you

but, like heav-en a - bove me,
that keeps me from run - nin',
the spy who loved me is
but just keep it com - in'.

keep-in' all my se-crets safe to - night.
How'd you learn to do the things you
do?
And

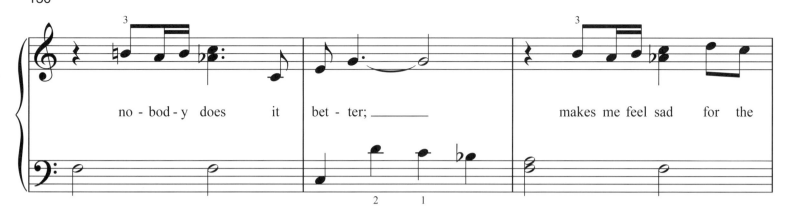

no - bod - y does it bet - ter; _____ makes me feel sad for the

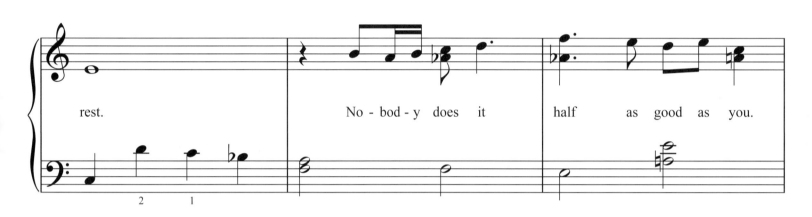

rest. No - bod - y does it half as good as you.

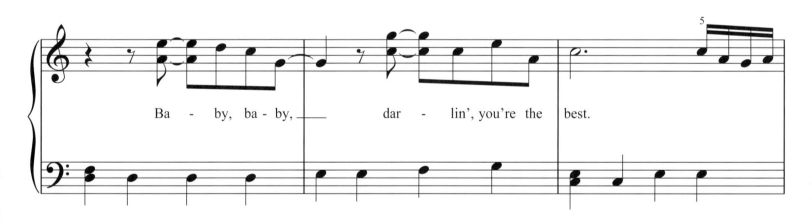

Ba - by, ba - by, _____ dar - lin', you're the best.

THE PINK PANTHER
from THE PINK PANTHER

By HENRY MANCINI

Moderately, mysteriously

OH, PRETTY WOMAN
featured in the Motion Picture PRETTY WOMAN

Words and Music by ROY ORBISON
and BILL DEES

Moderate Rock

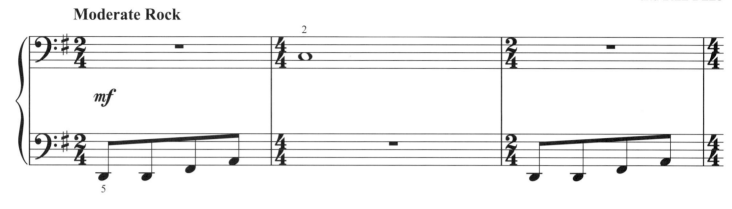

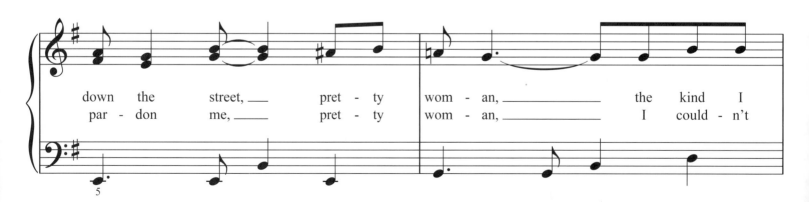

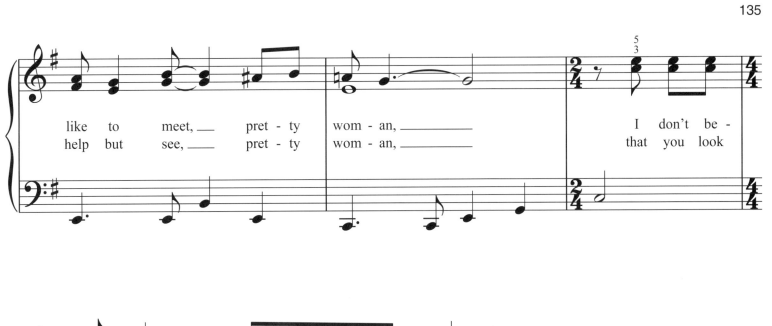

like to meet, ___ pret - ty wom - an, _____ I don't be -
help but see, ___ pret - ty wom - an, _____ that you look

lieve you, _____ you're not the truth; _____ no one could
love - ly _____ as can be; _____ are you

look as good as you.
lone - ly just like me?

Pret - ty

OLD TIME ROCK & ROLL

featured in RISKY BUSINESS

Words and Music by GEORGE JACKSON
and THOMAS E. JONES III

Moderate Rock 'n' Roll beat

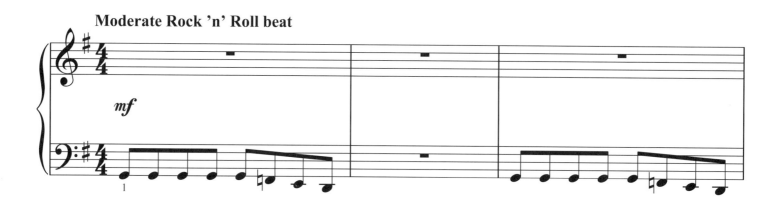

Just take those old rec-ords off the shelf. _ I'll sit and lis-ten to 'em
tan - go. _____

by my-self. I'd rath - er hear some blues or
funk-y old soul. To-day's mu-sic ain't got the same soul.
There's on-ly one sure way to get me to go;

I like that old - time _ rock 'n' roll. _ Don't try to take me to a
start play-ing old - time _ rock 'n' roll. _ Call me a re - lic. Call me

dis - co.
what you will.

You'll nev - er e - ven get me out on the floor.
Say I'm old - fash - ioned. Say I'm o - ver the hill.

In ten min - utes I'll be late for the door.
To - day's mu - sic ain't __ got the same soul.

I like that old time __
I like that old time __

rock 'n' roll. __
rock 'n' roll. __

Still like that old - time __ rock 'n' roll. __

That kind of mu - sic just soothes my soul. __ I rem - i - nisce a - bout the

days   of   old ___   with that old - time   rock 'n' roll. ___

1.

Won't go   to hear 'em play a

Still like that old - time _____ rock 'n' roll. _____

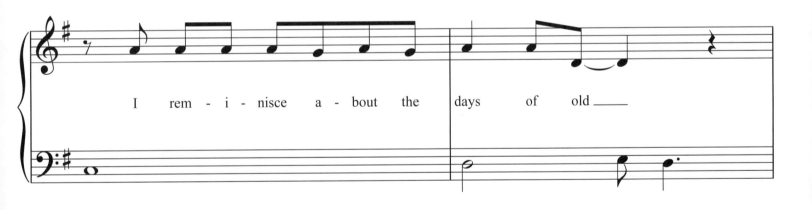

That kind of mu - sic just soothes my soul. _____

I rem - i - nisce a - bout the days of old _____

with that old - time rock 'n' roll. _____

PIECES OF DREAMS
(Little Boy Lost)
from the Motion Picture PIECES OF DREAMS

Lyrics by ALAN and MARILYN BERGMAN
Music by MICHEL LEGRAND

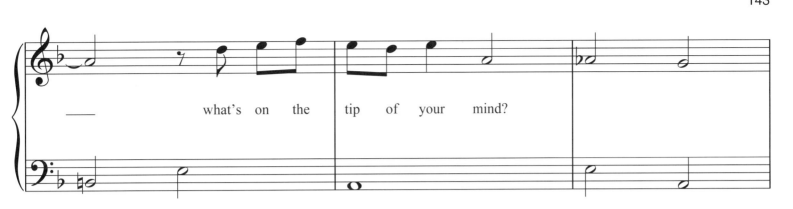

what's on the tip of your mind?

Why are you blind _____ to all you ev - er were, nev - er were,

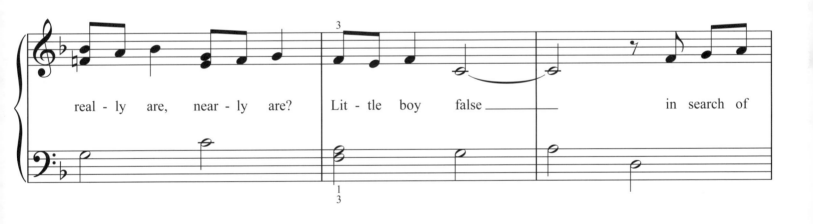

real - ly are, near - ly are? Lit - tle boy false _____ in search of

lit - tle boy true. _____ Will you be ev - er done trav - el - ing,

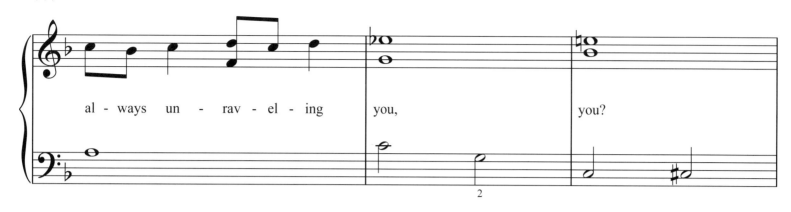

al - ways un - rav - el - ing you, you?

Run - ning a - way _____ could lead you fur - ther a - stray. _____

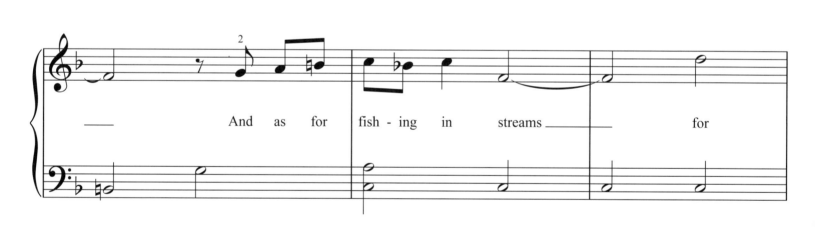

_____ And as for fish - ing in streams _____ for

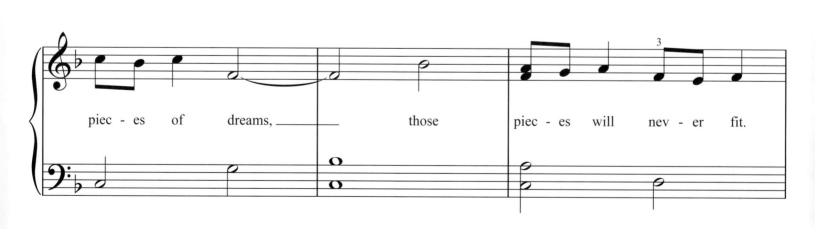

piec - es of dreams, _____ those piec - es will nev - er fit.

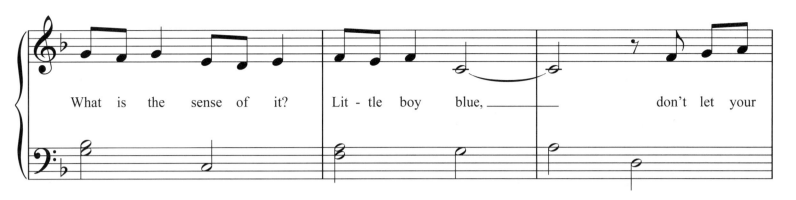

What is the sense of it? Lit - tle boy blue, _____ don't let your

lit - tle sheep roam. _____ It's time, come blow your horn, meet the morn,

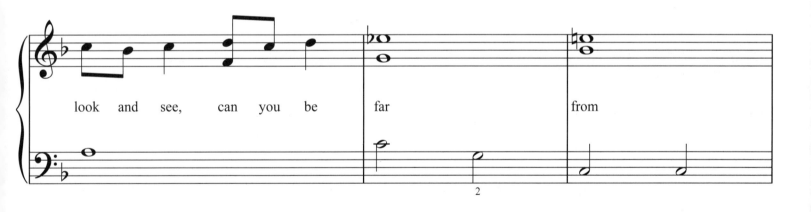

look and see, can you be far from

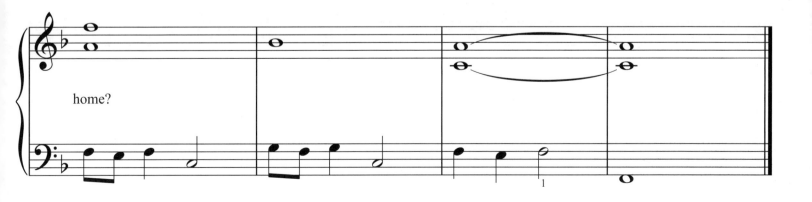

home?

RAIDERS MARCH
from RAIDERS OF THE LOST ARK

Music by JOHN WILLIAMS

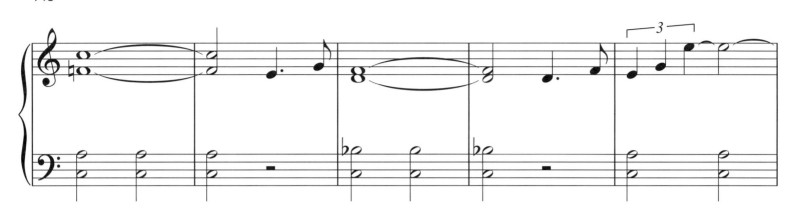

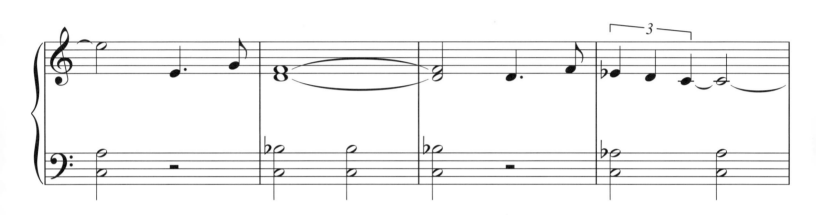

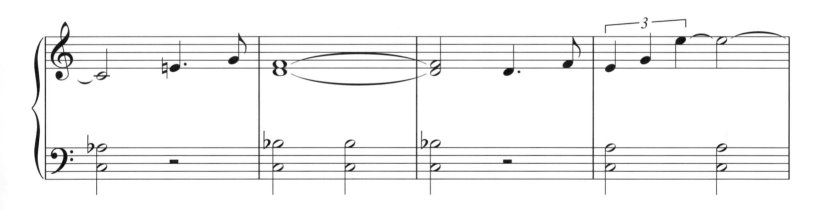

D.S. al Coda
(with repeat)

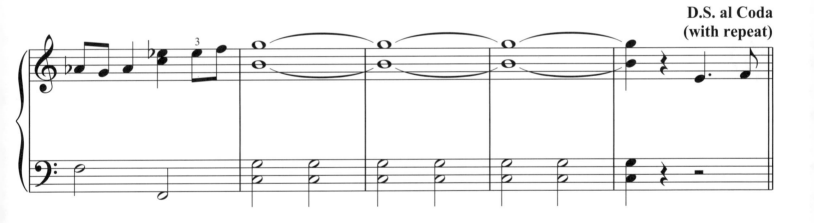

CODA

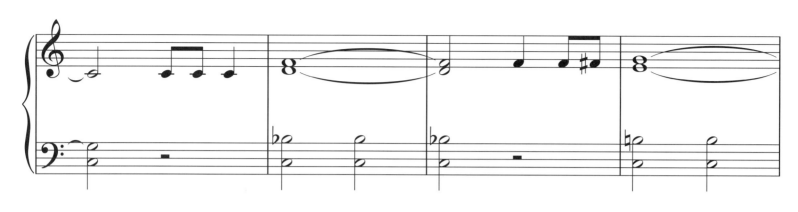

SOMEWHERE OUT THERE
from AN AMERICAN TAIL

Music by BARRY MANN
and JAMES HORNER
Lyric by CYNTHIA WEIL

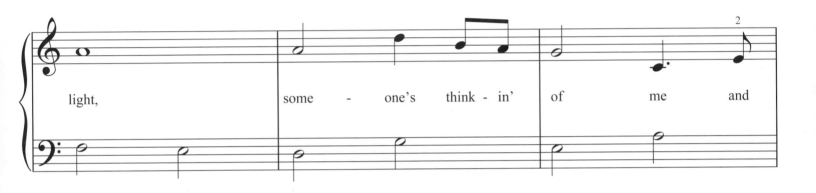

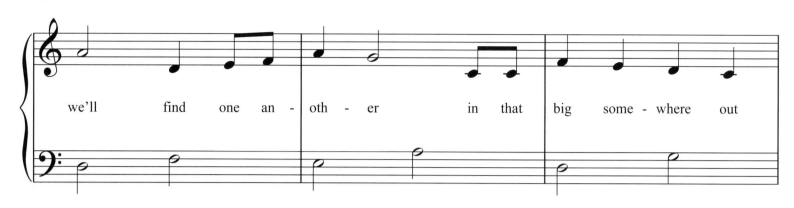

we'll   find   one   an -   oth -   er   in   that   big   some - where   out

there.   And   e - ven though I   know how ver - y   far   a - part we   are,   it

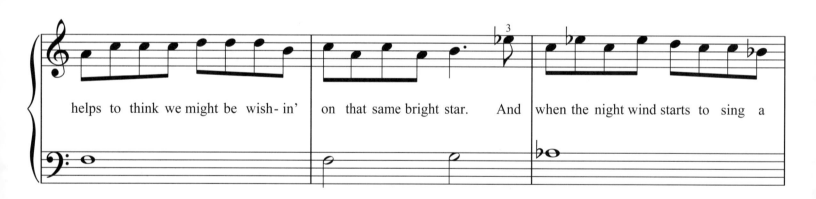

helps   to   think we might be   wish- in'   on   that same bright   star.   And   when the night wind starts to   sing   a

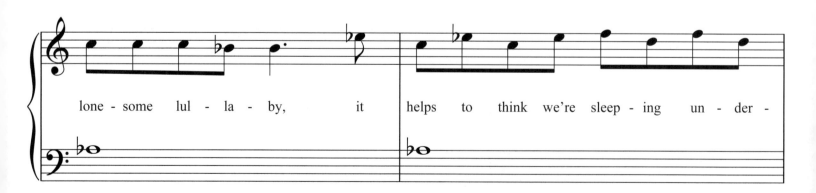

lone - some   lul - la - by,   it   helps   to   think   we're   sleep - ing   un - der-

neath the same big sky. *rit.* Some - where *a tempo* out there, if

love can see us through, then we'll be to -

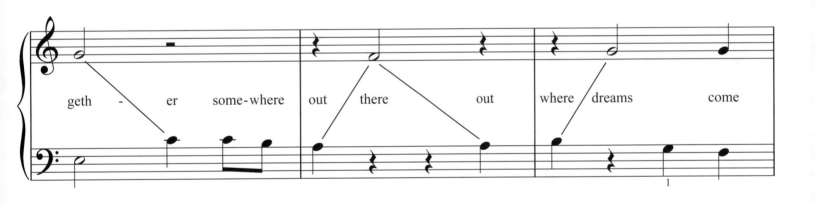

geth - er some-where out there out where dreams come

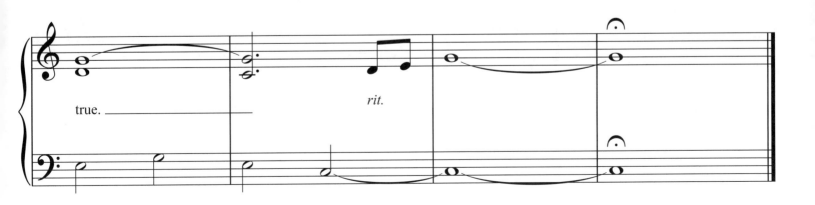

true. *rit.*

THE RAINBOW CONNECTION

from THE MUPPET MOVIE

Words and Music by PAUL WILLIAMS
and KENNETH L. ASCHER

Flowing Waltz

1. Why are there so man - y songs a - bout rain - bows, and
2. Who said that ev - 'ry wish would be heard and an - swered when
3. *(See additional lyrics)*

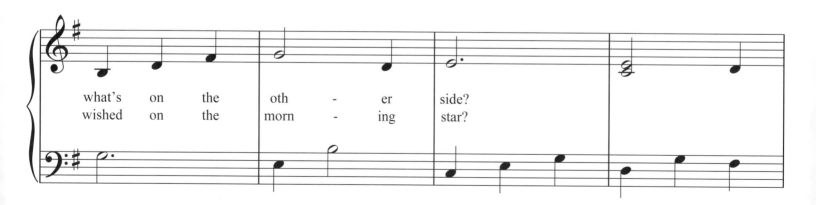

what's on the oth - er side?
wished on the morn - ing star?

155

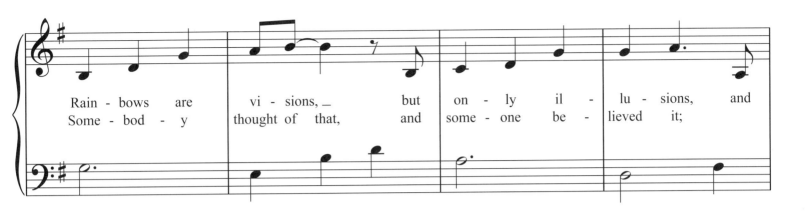

Rain - bows are vi - sions, __ but on - ly il - lu - sions, and
Some - bod - y thought of that, and some - one be - lieved it;

rain - bows have noth - ing to hide.
look what it's done __ so far.

So we've been told, and some choose to be - lieve it;
What's so a - maz - ing some that keeps us star - gaz - ing and

I know they're wrong; wait and see. __
what do we think we might see? __

Some - day we'll find it, the Rain - bow Con - nec - tion; the

To Coda ⊕

1.

lov - ers, the dream - ers ___ and me.

2.

me. All of us

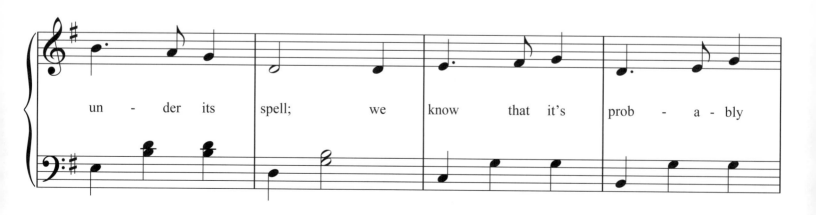

un - der its spell; we know that it's prob - a - bly

D.S. al Coda

mag - ic.

CODA

me.

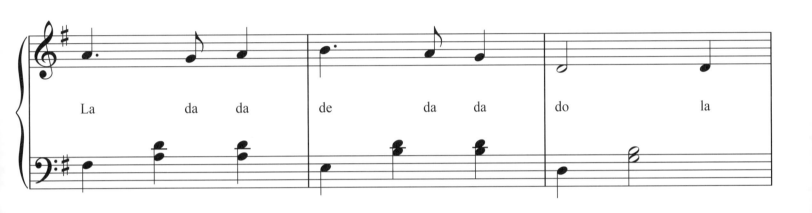

La da da de da da do la

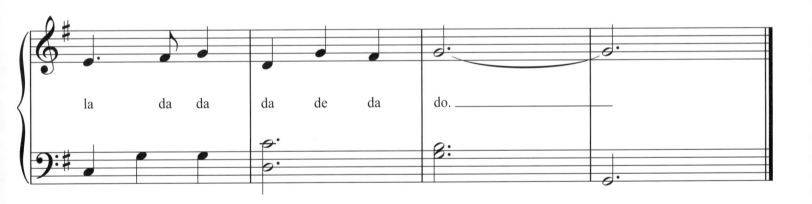

la da da da de da do. _____

Additional Lyrics

3. Have you been half asleep and have you heard voices?
   I've heard them calling my name.
   Is this the sweet sound that calls the young sailors?
   The voice might be one and the same.
   I've heard it too many times to ignore it.
   It's something that I'm s'posed to be.
   Someday we'll find it,
   The Rainbow Connection;
   The lovers, the dreamers and me.

REMEMBER ME
(Ernesto de la Cruz)
from COCO

Music and Lyrics by KRISTEN ANDERSON-LOPEZ
and ROBERT LOPEZ

Moderately fast

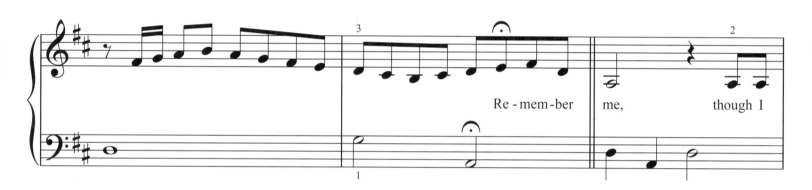

night we are a - part. Re - mem - ber me   though I   have to tra - vel far. Re - mem - ber

me   each time you   hear a sad gui - tar.   Know that I'm with you the on - ly

way that I can be.   Un - til you're in my arms a - gain,   re - mem - ber

me.

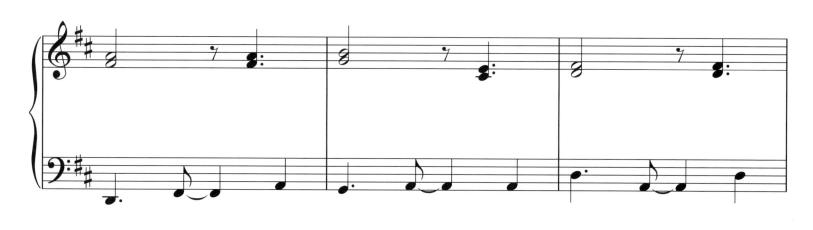

Re - mem - ber

me,   though I   have to   say good- bye. Re - mem- ber   me,   don't

let   it make you cry.   For   e - ven if I'm far a - way, __ I   hold you in my heart.   I

sing a se-cret song to you each night we are a-part. Re-mem - ber me though I

have to trav-el far. Re-mem-ber me each time you hear a sad gui-tar.

Slowly, deliberately

Know that I'm with you the on-ly way that I can be. *rall.* Un-til you're in my arms a-

gain, re - mem - ber me._____

SHALLOW
from A STAR IS BORN

Words and Music by STEFANI GERMANOTTA,
MARK RONSON, ANDREW WYATT
and ANTHONY ROSSOMANDO

Moderately

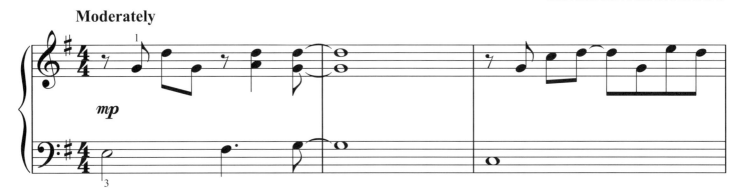

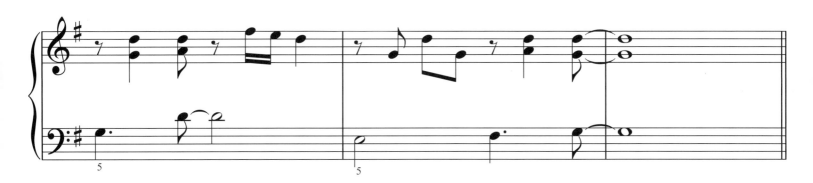

Tell me some-thing, girl: ___ are you hap-py in this
Tell me some-thing, boy: ___ aren't you tired, _ tryin' to

mod-ern world, _ or do you need more? ___
fill that void, _ or do you need more? ___

Is there some-thing that you're search-ing for? __ I'm fall - ing. __
Ain't it hard keep - ing it so hard - core? __

__ In all the good times I find my-self __ long - ing __

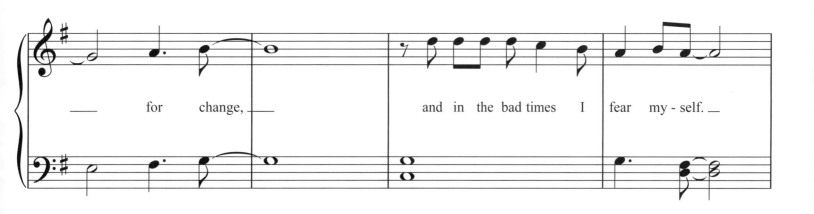

__ for change, __ and in the bad times I fear my - self. __

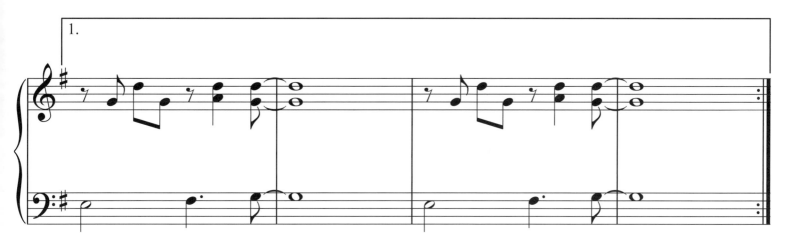

1.

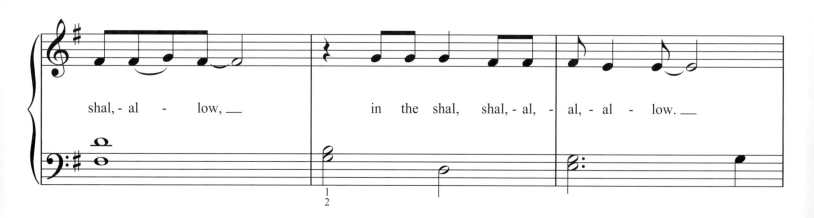

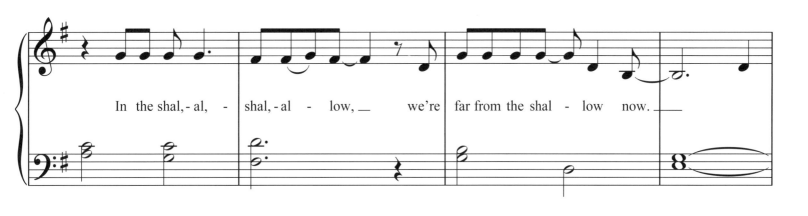

In the shal,- al, - shal,- al - low, __ we're far from the shal - low now. __

Oh, ah, __ __ ah, __ ah, __

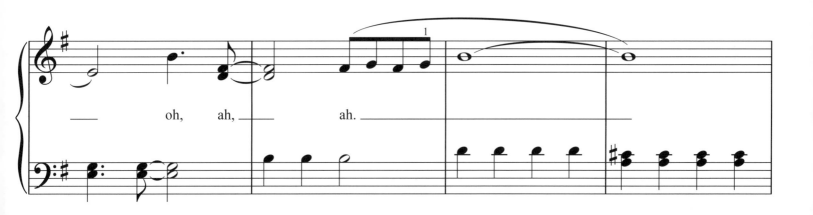

__ oh, ah, __ ah. __

I'm off the deep __ end. Watch as I dive __ in. I'll nev - er meet __ the ground. __

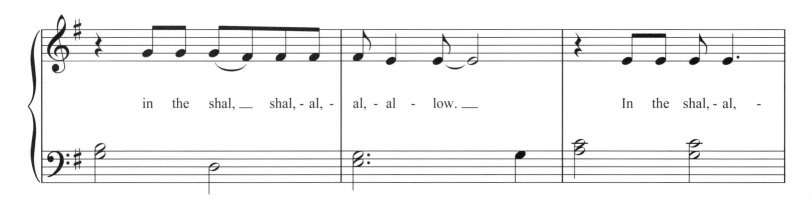

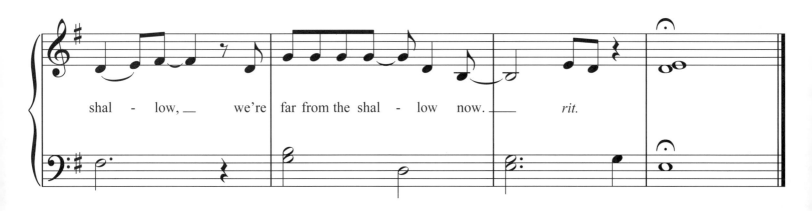

THIS IS ME
from THE GREATEST SHOWMAN

Words and Music by BENJ PASEK
and JUSTIN PAUL

Defiantly

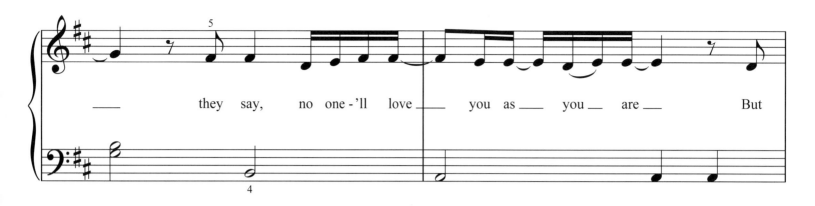

they say, no one-'ll love ___ you as ___ you ___ are ___ But

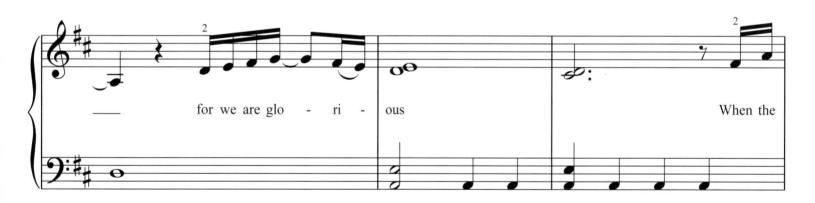

I won't let them break me down ___ to dust   I know that there's a place ___ for us, ___

___ for we are glo - ri - ous   When the

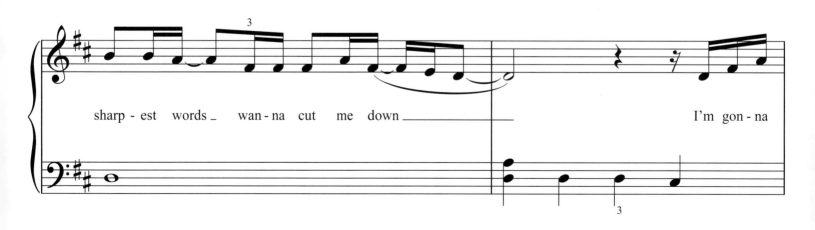

sharp - est words ___ wan - na cut me down _____   I'm gon - na

send a flood, gon-na drown 'em out _____ I am brave, I am bruised I am who ___

____ I'm meant _ to be This is me Look out, __ 'cause here __ I come; _____

____ and I'm march - in' on to the beat I drum _____

____ I'm not scared to be seen I make no ___ a-pol-o-gies This is me

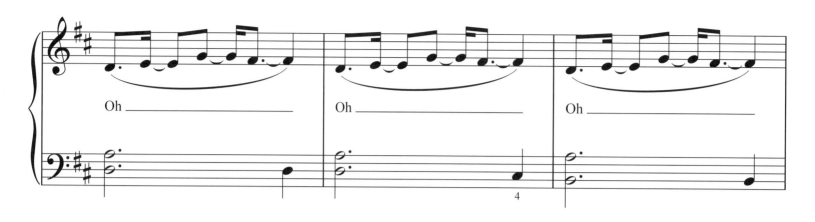

Oh _____ Oh _____ Oh _____

To Coda ⊕

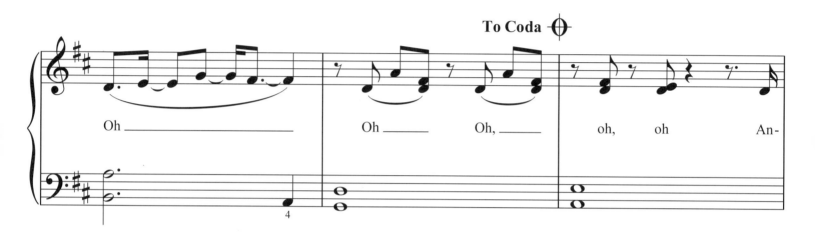

Oh _____ Oh _____ Oh, _____ oh, oh An-

oth - er round of bul-lets hits my skin   Well, fi - re a - way, ____ 'cause to-day   I won't let ____

____ the shame _ sink _ in ____   We are   burst - in' through the bar - ri - cades _ and

D.S. al Coda

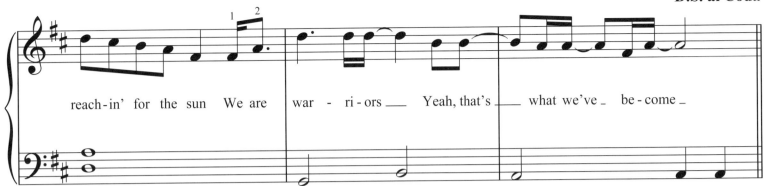

reach-in' for the sun We are war - ri - ors ___ Yeah, that's ___ what we've ___ be - come ___

CODA

oh, oh This is me Oh _____

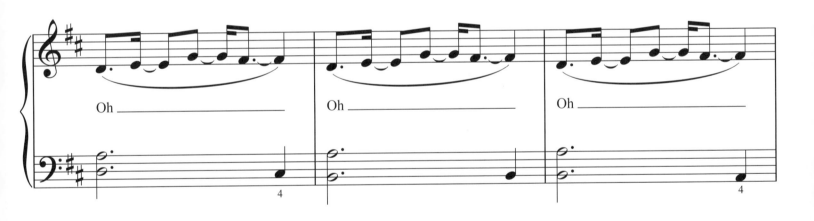

Oh _____ Oh _____ Oh _____

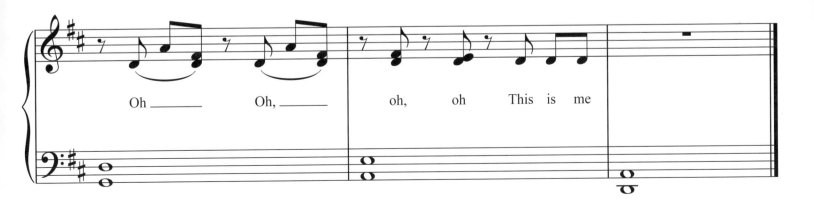

Oh _____ Oh, _____ oh, oh This is me

SOMEWHERE IN MY MEMORY

from the Twentieth Century Fox Motion Picture HOME ALONE

Words by LESLIE BRICUSSE
Music by JOHN WILLIAMS

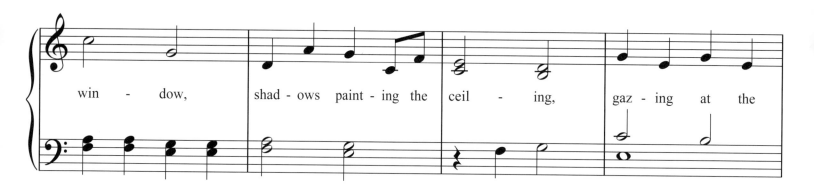

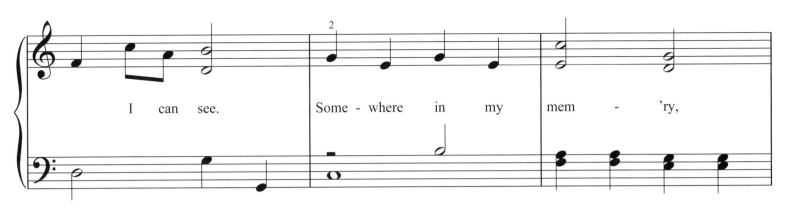

I can see. Some - where in my mem - 'ry,

Christ - mas joys all a - round me, liv - ing in my mem - 'ry,

all of the mu - sic, all of the mag - ic, all of the fam - 'ly

home here with me.

STAR WARS
(Main Theme)
from STAR WARS: A NEW HOPE

Music by JOHN WILLIAMS

Majestically

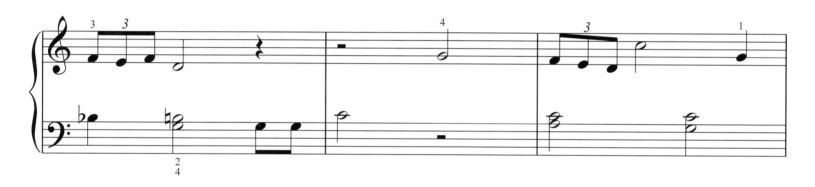

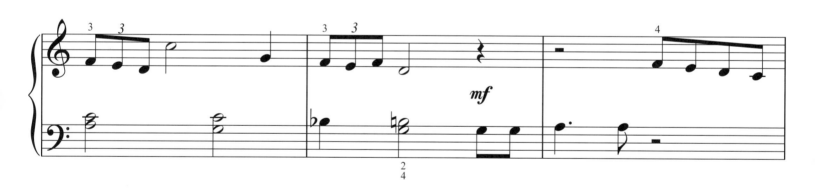

SONG FROM M*A*S*H
(Suicide Is Painless)
from M*A*S*H

Words and Music by MIKE ALTMAN
and JOHNNY MANDEL

Moderately fast

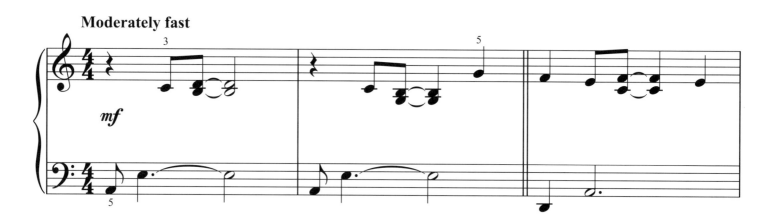

TARA'S THEME
(My Own True Love)
from GONE WITH THE WIND

By MAX STEINER

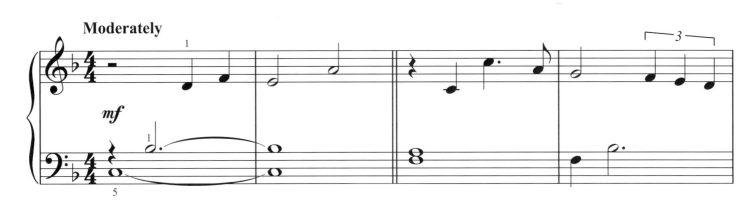

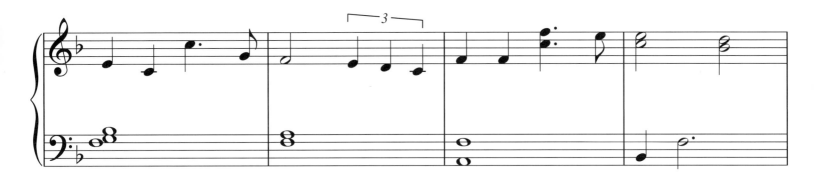

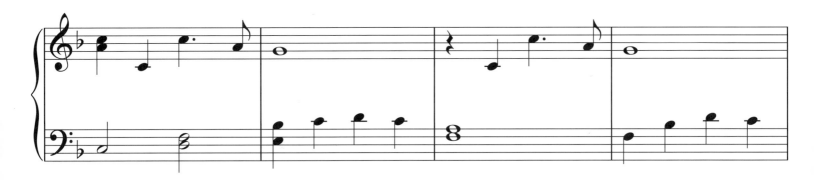

THAT'S WHAT FRIENDS ARE FOR

from NIGHT SHIFT

Music by BURT BACHARACH
Words by CAROLE BAYER SAGER

Instrumental

I nev - er thought I'd feel this way and as far as I'm con-
Well, you came and o - pened

cerned I'm glad I got ___ the chance ___ to say ___ that I do be - lieve ___ I
me and now there's so ___ much more ___ I see; ___ and so, by the way, ___ I

181

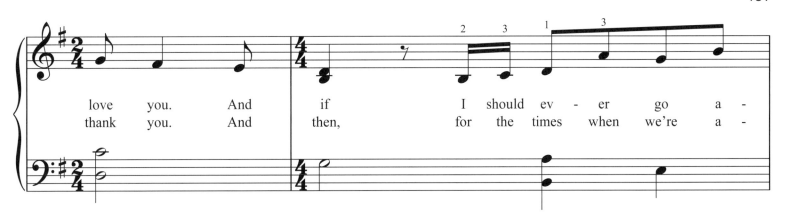

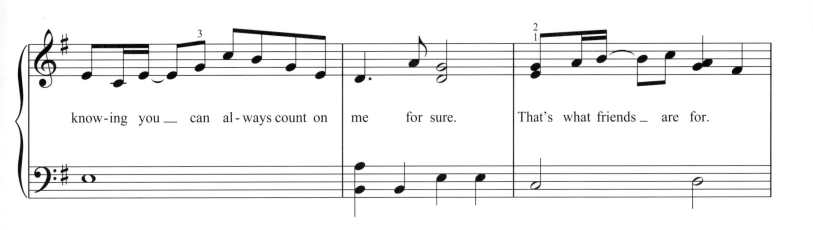

In good _ times and bad _ times, I'll be on ___ your side for - ev - er - more.

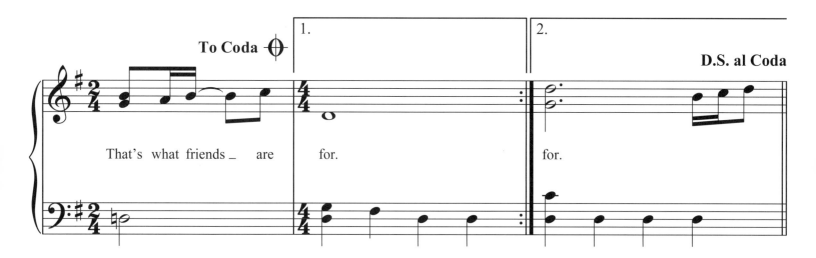

To Coda ⊕ | 1. | 2.   **D.S. al Coda**

That's what friends _ are   for.   for.

CODA
⊕

for.

WHAT THE WORLD NEEDS NOW IS LOVE

featured in ARTHUR

Lyric by HAL DAVID
Music by BURT BACHARACH

With a Jazz Waltz swing

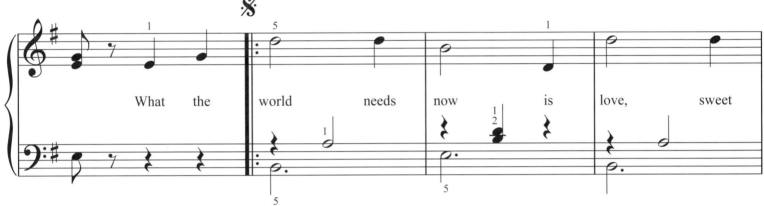

What the world needs now is love, sweet

love. It's the on-ly thing ____ that there's just too

lit-tle of. What the world needs now is love, sweet

184

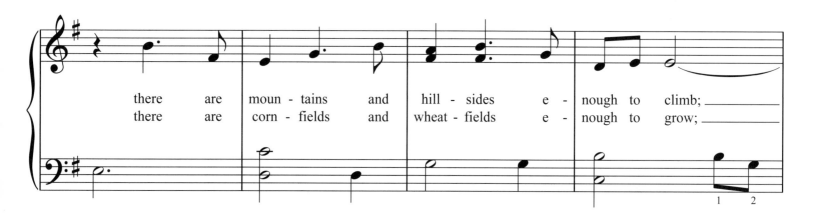

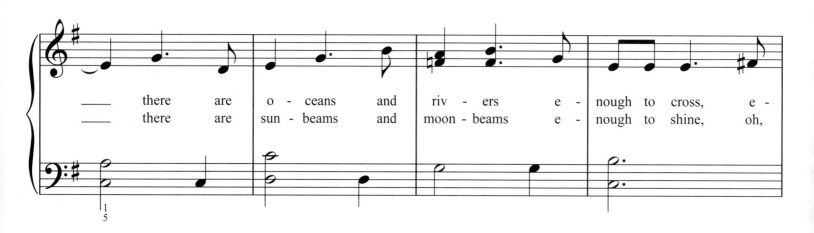

TIME WARP
from THE ROCKY HORROR PICTURE SHOW

Words and Music by
RICHARD O'BRIEN

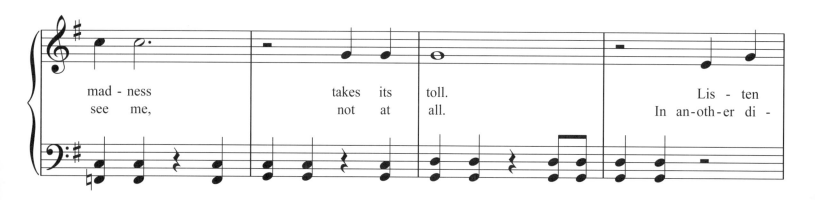

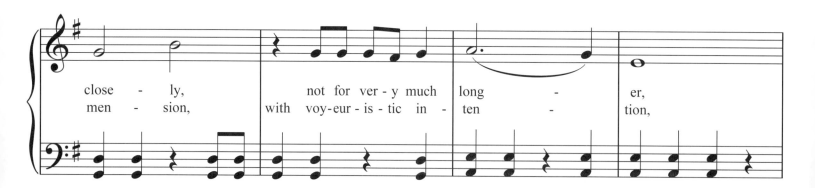

I've got to keep ____ con - trol. ____ I re -
well se - clud-ed I'll ____ see all. ____ With a bit of a

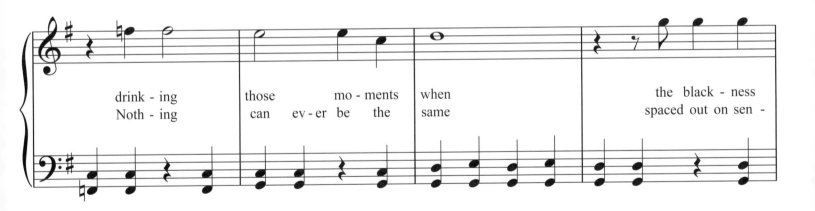

mem - ber ___ do - ing the Time Warp, ____
mind flip, ___ you're in - to the time slip. ____

drink - ing those mo - ments when the black - ness
Noth - ing can ev - er be the same spaced out on sen -

hits me ___ and the void would be call - ing.}
sa - tion ___ like you're un - der se - da - tion.}

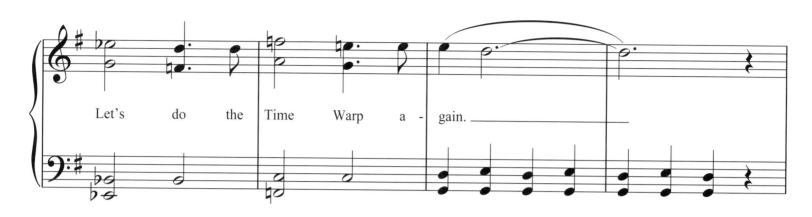

Let's   do   the   Time   Warp   a - gain.

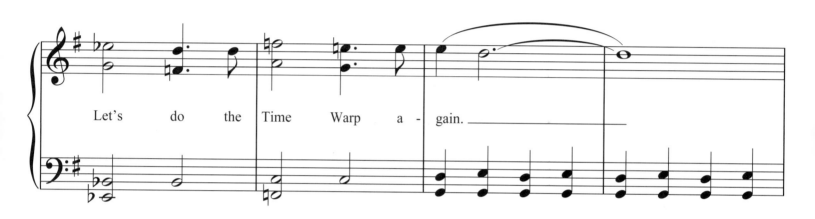

Let's   do   the   Time   Warp   a - gain.

It's just a jump to the   left   and then a step to the   right.

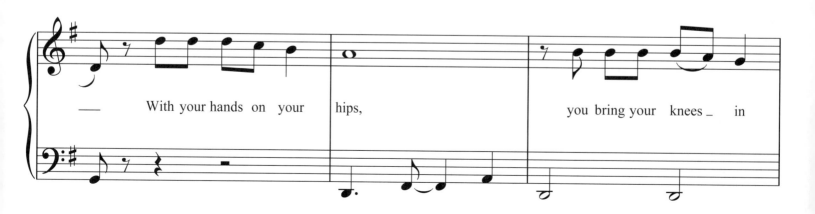

— With your hands on your   hips,   you bring your   knees _   in

tight.   But it's the pel - vic   thrusts _____

that real - ly drive you in - sane. _____   Let's do the

Time Warp a - gain. _____   Let's do the

Time Warp a - gain. _____   It's so

THE TROLLEY SONG
from MEET ME IN ST. LOUIS

Words and Music by HUGH MARTIN
and RALPH BLANE

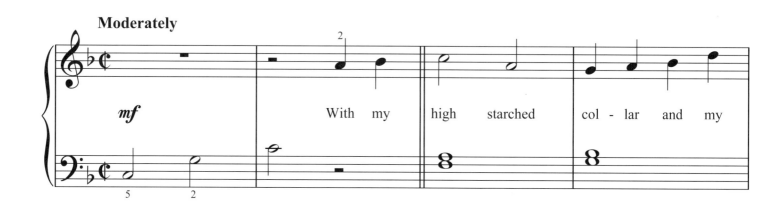

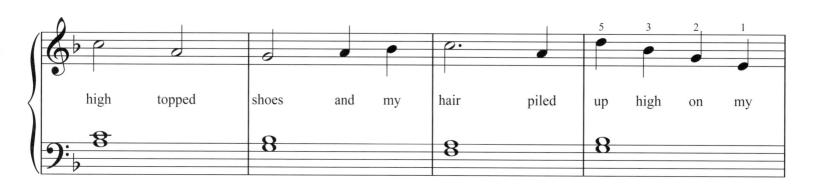

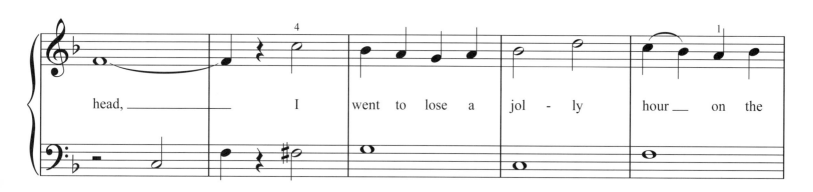

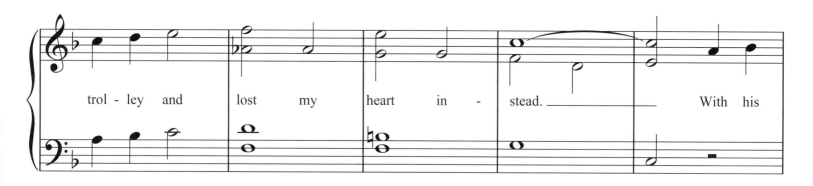

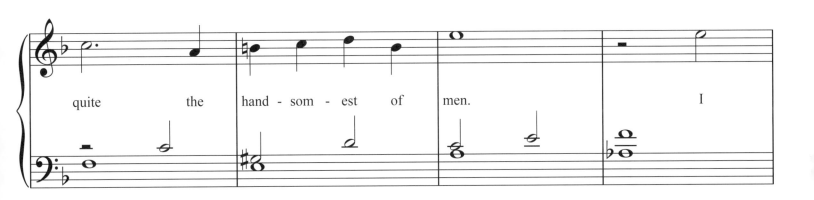

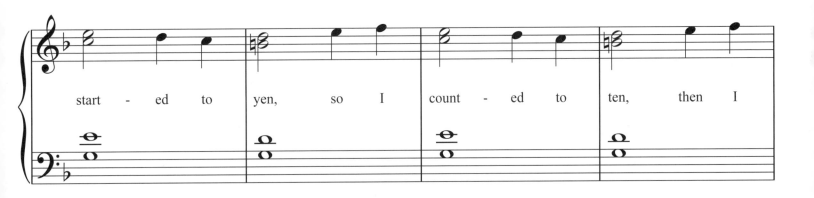

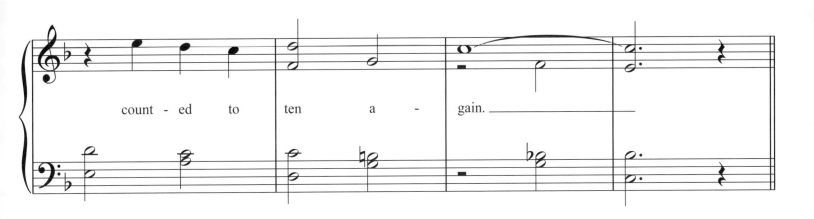

192

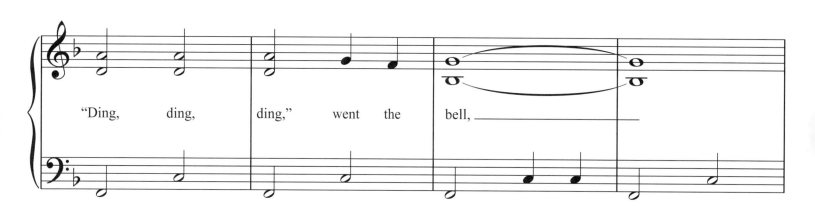

"Chug, chug, chug," went the

mo - tor, _____ "Bump, bump, bump," went the

brake, _____ "Thump, thump, thump," went my

heart - strings, _____ when he smiled I could feel the car

194

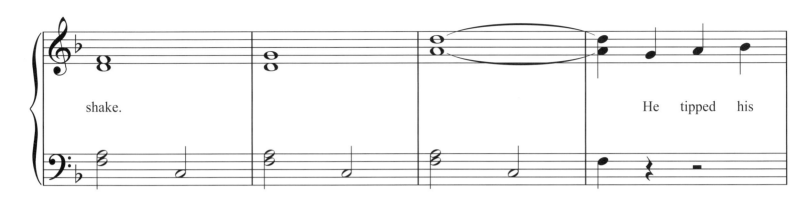

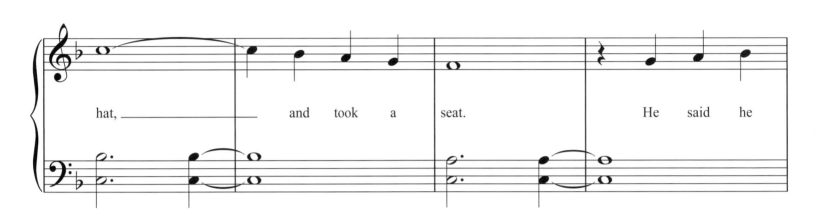

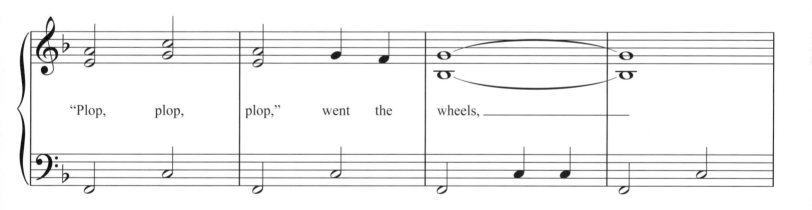

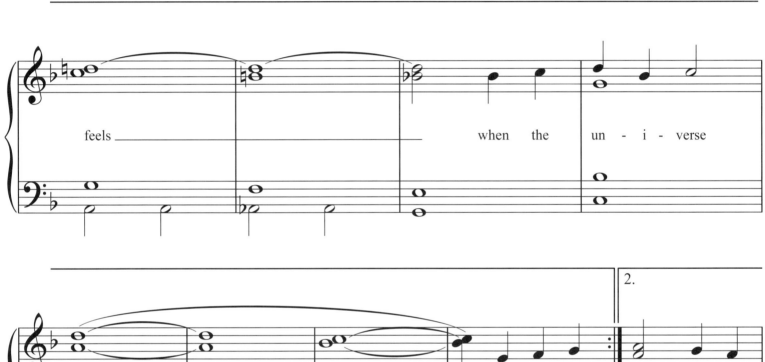

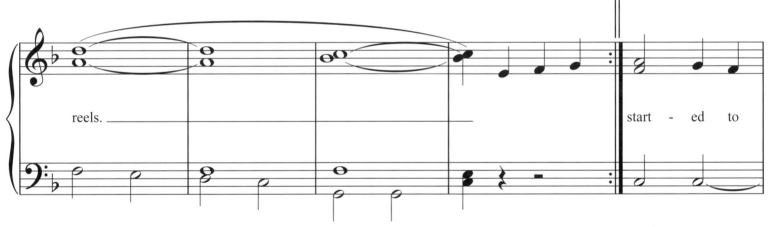

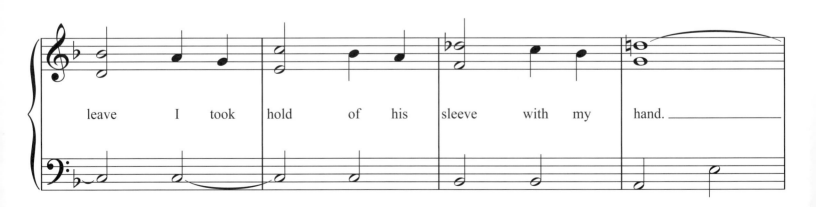

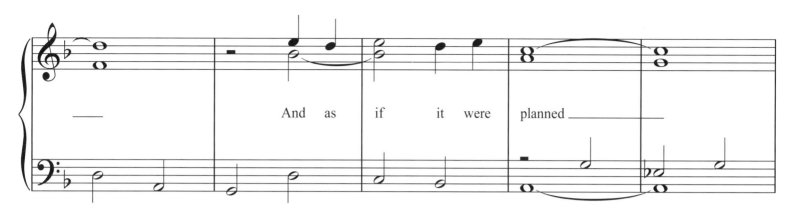

And as if it were planned

he stayed on with me and it was grand, just to

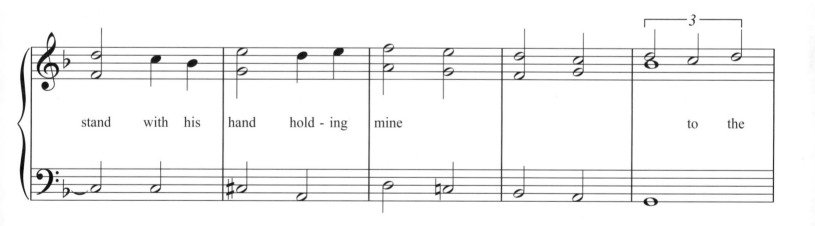

stand with his hand hold-ing mine to the

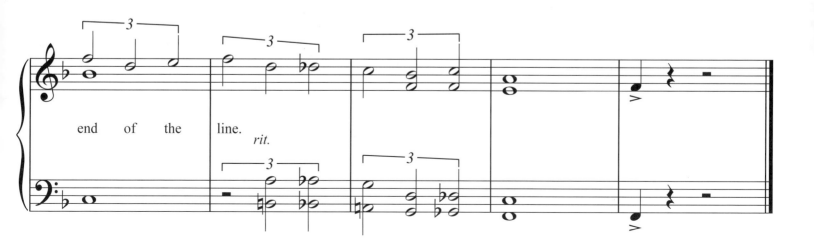

end of the line. *rit.*

TWIST AND SHOUT

featured in the Motion Picture FERRIS BUELLER'S DAY OFF

Words and Music by BERT RUSSELL
and PHIL MEDLEY

Moderately, with a beat

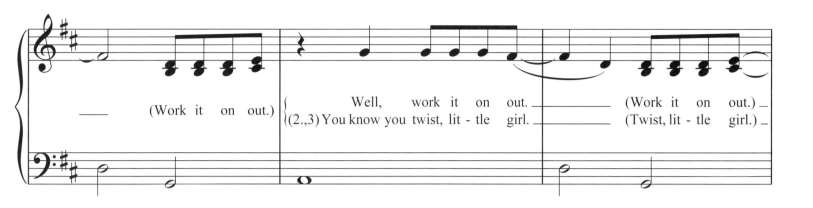

(Work it on out.)   Well,   work it on out.   (Work it on out.)
(2.,3) You know you twist, lit - tle girl.   (Twist, lit - tle girl.)

You know you look so good. (Look so good.)   You know you got   me
You know you twist so fine. (Twist so fine.)   Come on and twist a lit - tle

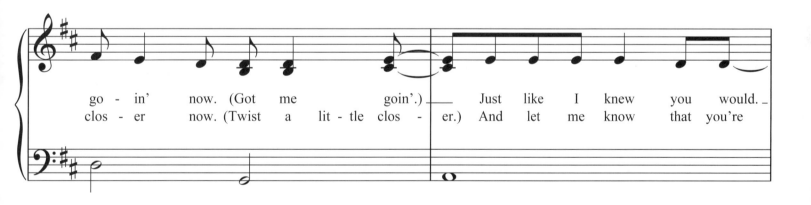

go - in' now. (Got me goin'.)   Just like I knew you would.
clos - er now. (Twist a lit - tle clos - er.) And let me know that you're

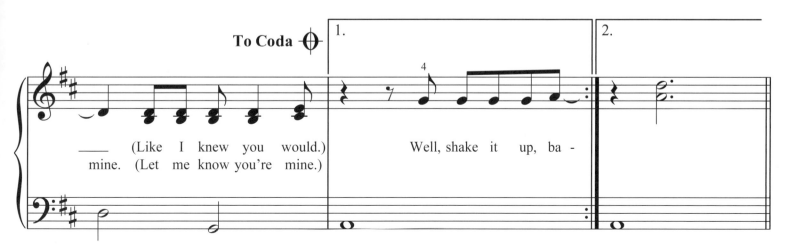

To Coda ⊕   1.   2.

(Like I knew you would.)   Well, shake it up, ba -
mine. (Let me know you're mine.)

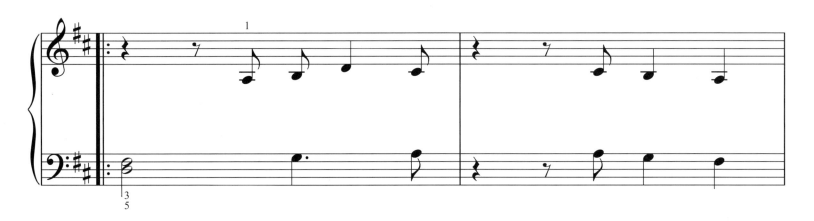

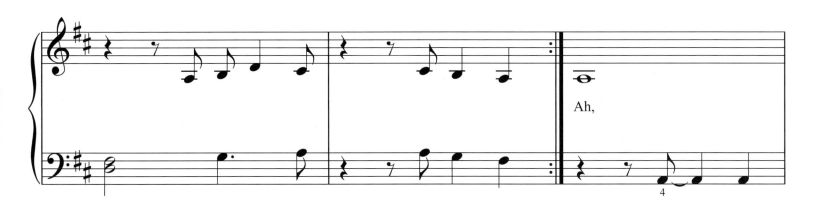

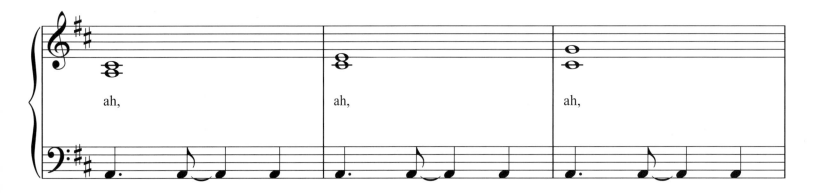

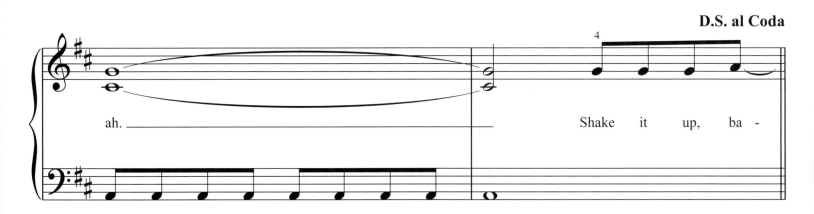

CODA

Well, shake it, shake it, shake it, ba - by, now. (Shake it up, babe.)

Well, shake it, shake it, shake it ba - by, now. (Shake it up, babe.)

Oo. Ah, ah,

ah, ah.

THE WINDMILLS OF YOUR MIND
Theme from THE THOMAS CROWN AFFAIR

Words by ALAN and MARILYN BERGMAN
Music by MICHEL LEGRAND

Moderately, freely

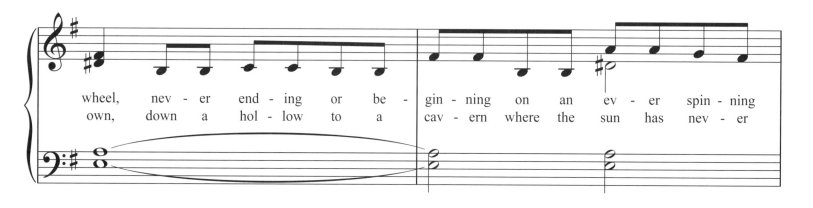

Round like a cir-cle in a spi-ral, like a wheel with-in a
mind! Like a tun-nel that you fol-low to a tun-nel of its

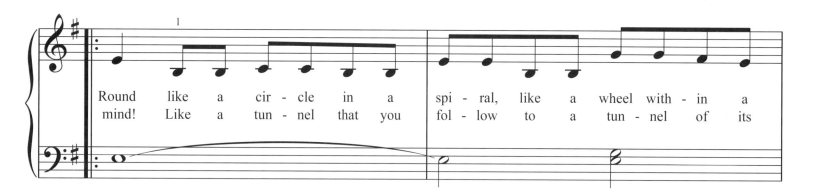

wheel, nev-er end-ing or be-gin-ning on an ev-er spin-ning
own, down a hol-low to a cav-ern where the sun has nev-er

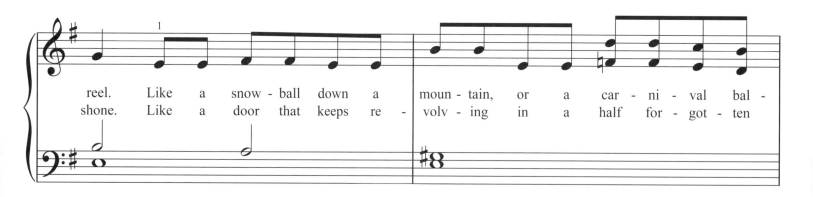

reel. Like a snow-ball down a moun-tain, or a car-ni-val bal-
shone. Like a door that keeps re-volv-ing in a half for-got-ten

203

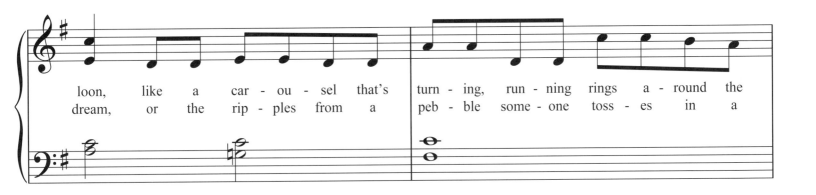

loon, like a car - ou - sel that's turn - ing, run - ning rings a - round the
dream, or the rip - ples from a peb - ble some - one toss - es in a

moon.
stream. } Like a clock whose hands are sweep - ing past the min - utes of its

face, and the world is like an ap - ple whirl - ing si - lent - ly in

space, like the cir - cles that you find in the wind - mills of your

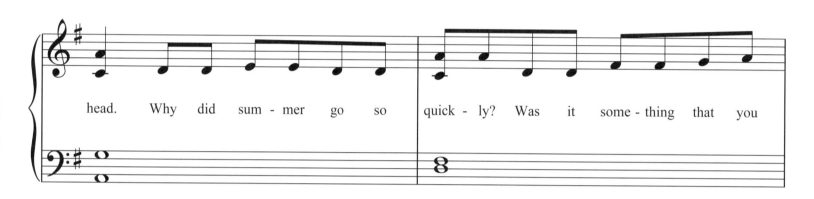

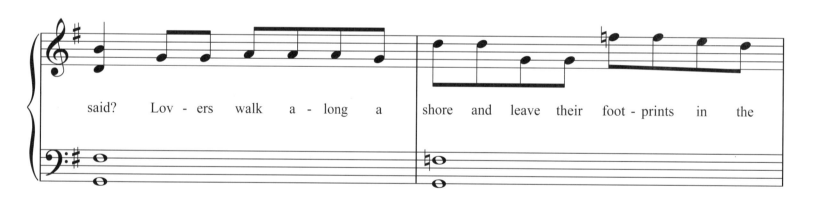

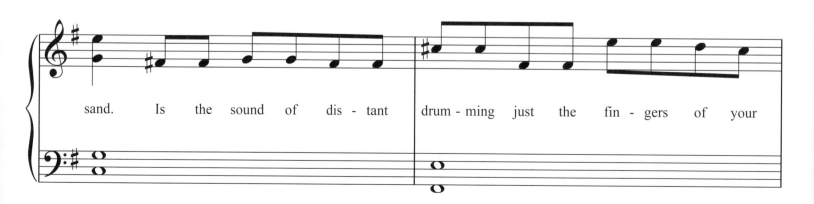

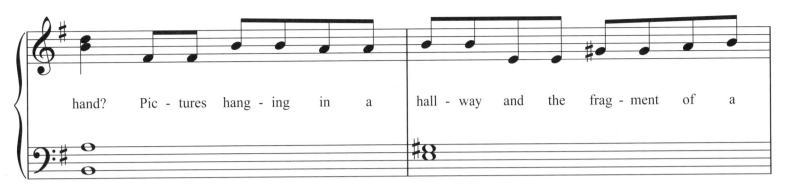

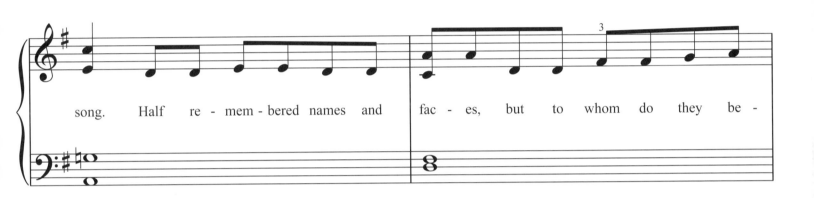

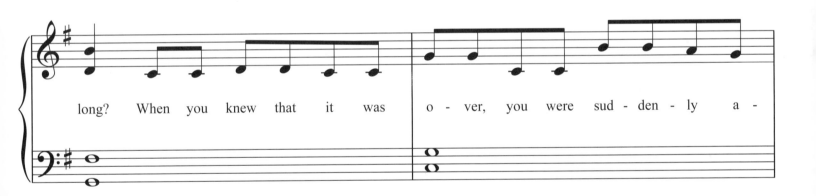

hair! Like a cir - cle in a spi - ral, like a wheel with - in a wheel, nev - er end - ing or be -

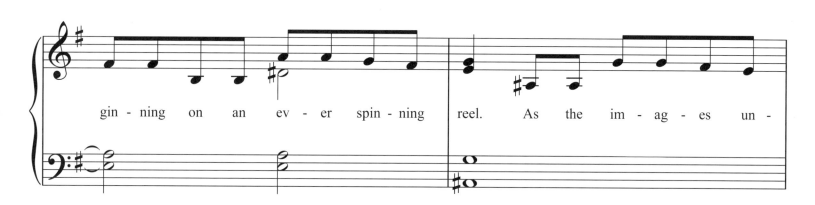

gin - ning on an ev - er spin - ning reel. As the im - ag - es un -

wind, like the cir - cles that you find in the wind-mills of your mind!

poco rit.   *a tempo*

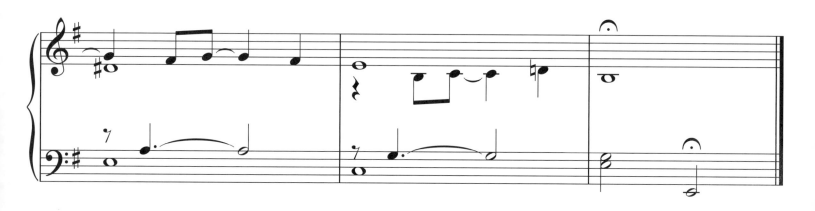

FIRST 50

You've been taking lessons, you've got a few chords under your belt, and you're ready to buy a songbook. Now what?
*Hal Leonard has the answers in its **First 50** series.*

These books contain easy to intermediate arrangements with lyrics for must-know songs.
Each arrangement is simple and streamlined, yet still captures the essence of the tune.

First 50 Acoustic Songs You Should Play on Piano
00293416 Easy Piano.........................$16.99

First 50 Baroque Pieces You Should Play on Piano
00291453 Easy Piano.........................$14.99

First 50 Songs by the Beatles You Should Play on the Piano
00172236 Easy Piano.......................$19.99

First 50 Broadway Songs You Should Play on the Piano
00150167 Easy Piano.........................$14.99

First 50 Christmas Carols You Should Play on the Piano
00147216 Easy Piano.........................$14.99

First 50 Christmas Songs You Should Play on the Piano
00172041 Easy Piano.........................$14.99

First 50 Classic Rock Songs You Should Play on Piano
00195619 Easy Piano.......................$16.99

First 50 Classical Pieces You Should Play on the Piano
00131436 Easy Piano Solo................$14.99

First 50 Country Songs You Should Play on the Piano
00150166 Easy Piano.........................$14.99

First 50 Disney Songs You Should Play on the Piano
00274938 Easy Piano.........................$16.99

First 50 Early Rock Songs You Should Play on the Piano
00160570 Easy Piano.........................$14.99

First 50 Folk Songs You Should Play on the Piano
00235867 Easy Piano.........................$14.99

First 50 4-Chord Songs You Should Play on the Piano
00249562 Easy Piano.........................$16.99

First 50 Gospel Songs You Should Play on Piano
00282526 Easy Piano.........................$14.99

First 50 Hymns You Should Play on Piano
00275199 Easy Piano.........................$14.99

First 50 Jazz Standards You Should Play on Piano
00196269 Easy Piano.........................$14.99

First 50 Kids' Songs You Should Play on Piano
00196071 Easy Piano.........................$14.99

First 50 Latin Songs You Should Play on the Piano
00248747 Easy Piano.........................$16.99

First 50 Movie Songs You Should Play on the Piano
00150165 Easy Piano.........................$16.99

First 50 Movie Themes You Should Play on Piano
00278368 Easy Piano.........................$16.99

First 50 Songs You Should Play on the Organ
00288203 ....$19.99

First 50 Piano Duets You Should Play
00276571 1 Piano, 4 Hands...............$19.99

First 50 Pop Ballads You Should Play on the Piano
00248987 Easy Piano.........................$16.99

First 50 Pop Hits You Should Play on the Piano
00234374 Easy Piano.........................$16.99

First 50 Popular Songs You Should Play on the Piano
00131140 Easy Piano.........................$16.99

First 50 R&B Songs You Should Play on Piano
00196028 Easy Piano.........................$14.99

First 50 3-Chord Songs You Should Play on Piano
00249666 Easy Piano.........................$16.99

First 50 Worship Songs You Should Play on Piano
00287138 Easy Piano.........................$16.99

HAL•LEONARD®

www.halleonard.com

Prices, content and availability subject to change without notice.

THE NEW DECADE SERIES
EASY PIANO EDITIONS

The New Decade series books contain 80–100 iconic songs from each decade creating a complete historical library of popular music. These easy piano editions feature straightforward piano arrangements with lyrics.

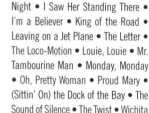

SONGS OF THE 1920s
Among My Souvenirs • April Showers • Button up Your Overcoat • Bye Bye Blackbird • California, Here I Come • I'll See You in My Dreams • It Had to Be You • Let a Smile Be Your Umbrella • Look for the Silver Lining • Mack the Knife • Makin' Whoopee! • The Man I Love • My Blue Heaven • Puttin' on the Ritz • St. Louis Blues • Side by Side • Sleepy Time Gal • Stardust • Swanee • Yes Sir, That's My Baby • and more.
00282474..............................$24.99

SONGS OF THE 1930s
As Time Goes By • Blue Moon • Body and Soul • Embraceable You • Georgia on My Mind • The Glory of Love • I Don't Know Why (I Just Do) • I Got Rhythm • I'll Be Seeing You • In the Mood • The Lady Is a Tramp • Love Is Here to Stay • Mood Indigo • My Funny Valentine • The Nearness of You • Over the Rainbow • Sing, Sing, Sing • Summertime • The Very Thought of You • The Way You Look Tonight • and more.
00282475...........................$24.99

SONGS OF THE 1940s
Ac-cent-tchu-ate the Positive • Bésame Mucho (Kiss Me Much) • Boogie Woogie Bugle Boy • Don't Get Around Much Anymore • How High the Moon • I Get a Kick Out of You • It Might As Well Be Spring • Moonlight in Vermont • A Nightingale Sang in Berkeley Square • Route 66 • Sentimental Journey • Time After Time • When You Wish upon a Star • You'd Be So Nice to Come Home To • Zip-A-Dee-Doo-Dah • and more.
00282476...........................$24.99

SONGS OF THE 1950s
All I Have to Do Is Dream • Bye Bye Love • Chantilly Lace • Don't Be Cruel • Earth Angel • Fever • Great Balls of Fire • Hound Dog • I Walk the Line • It's So Easy • Kansas City • Lonely Teardrops • Mister Sandman • Only You (And You Alone) • Peter Gunn • Rock Around the Clock • Shout • Sixteen Tons • Tequila • Unchained Melody • Volare • Why Do Fools Fall in Love • Yakety Yak • Your Cheatin' Heart • and more.
00282477..............................$24.99

SONGS OF THE 1960s
Aquarius • Blowin' in the Wind • Do Wah Diddy Diddy • Downtown • God Only Knows • Good Vibrations • Happy Together • A Hard Day's Night • I Saw Her Standing There • I'm a Believer • King of the Road • Leaving on a Jet Plane • The Letter • The Loco-Motion • Louie, Louie • Mr. Tambourine Man • Monday, Monday • Oh, Pretty Woman • Proud Mary • (Sittin' On) the Dock of the Bay • The Sound of Silence • The Twist • Wichita Lineman • Wild Thing • and more.
00282478..............................$24.99

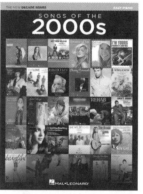

SONGS OF THE 1970s
ABC • American Pie • Bridge over Troubled Water • (They Long to Be) Close to You • Dancing Queen • Free Bird • Goodbye Yellow Brick Road • How Deep Is Your Love • I Shot the Sheriff • I Will Survive • Imagine • Killing Me Softly with His Song • Layla • Lean on Me • Maybe I'm Amazed • Piano Man • Reeling in the Years • Smoke on the Water • Stairway to Heaven • Stayin' Alive • Sweet Home Alabama • Time in a Bottle • Walk This Way • We Will Rock You • Y.M.C.A. • and more.
00282479..........................$24.99

SONGS OF THE 1980s
Another Brick in the Wall • Billie Jean • Chariots of Fire • Don't Stop Believin' • Endless Love • Eye of the Tiger • Flashdance... What a Feeling • How Will I Know • I Love Rock 'N Roll • Jump • Missing You • Nothing's Gonna Stop Us Now • Pour Some Sugar on Me • Right Here Waiting • Sweet Child O' Mine • Take on Me • Time After Time • Up Where We Belong • What's Love Got to Do with It • With or Without You • and more.
00282480..............................$24.99

SONGS OF THE 1990s
Always Be My Baby • As Long As You Love Me • Black Velvet • Can You Feel the Love Tonight • Dreams • Fields of Gold • Friends in Low Places • Good Riddance (Time of Your Life) • How Am I Supposed to Live Without You • I Need to Know • I'm the Only One • Ironic • Livin' La Vida Loca • Losing My Religion • More Than Words • Only Wanna Be with You • Smells like Teen Spirit • Smooth • Tears in Heaven • Under the Bridge • You're Still the One • and more.
00282481..............................$24.99

SONGS OF THE 2000s
Beautiful • Before He Cheats • Bye Bye Bye • Chasing Pavements • Don't Know Why • Drive • Fallin' • Hey There Delilah • I Gotta Feeling • I'm Yours • Just Dance • Love Story • Mercy • Only Time • The Reason • Rehab • This Love • A Thousand Miles • Umbrella • Viva La Vida • Waiting on the World to Change • With Arms Wide Open • You Raise Me Up • and more.
00282482..............................$24.99

SONGS OF THE 2010s
All About That Bass • Bad Romance • Brave • Call Me Maybe • Cups (When I'm Gone) • Feel It Still • Get Lucky • Happy • Havana • Hey, Soul Sister • I Will Wait • Just Give Me a Reason • Let It Go • Mean • Moves like Jagger • Need You Now • Radioactive • Rolling in the Deep • Shake It Off • Stay with Me • Thinking Out Loud • Uptown Funk • We Are Young • and more.
00282483..............................$24.99

Prices, contents, and availability subject to change without notice.

HAL•LEONARD®
www.halleonard.com

0219
041